~A Night Spent with Poetry~

Written by: Michael J.H. Messiano
Michael J. Housley

"Look to the eyes of those you love, and through their reflections you will find a poem."

~Michael J.H. Messiano~

ISBN 978-1-257-62310-5

ACKNOWLEDGEMENTS

I would like to express my deepest appreciation to my entire family, whom has been there for me since the birth of my writing began long ago. They continually and convincingly convey a strong loving spirit, which resembles my writing to its truest art form. Without their guidance and moral support I would not be able to do what I do best, which is to write. Their love and support is the key in all that's best in me.

In addition to crafting my skills as a writer, I would like to give a warm thanks to my late grandfather. His wisdom and knowledge has passed itself on to me as a young man. His presence in my life has left trails of dignity and self-respect to form a man in his image.

-The Color Blue- Act I

The battle begins when blue night turns into its darkest form…

"Abiri the Vanquisher"

O' kingly kings,
Who sit in clout upon your thrones;
I will not bow to you,
Not today, nor any other!

O' mighty rulers of all these things;
The land, the streams, and our homes.
I have come forth with courage too;
To say, that I stand in nobility to our lands, our mother!

O' this day is yours and not ours,
Nevertheless, I will still fight,
But the glory that comes dusk shall be the countrymen's-
Before my last breath upon these plains!

O' under this rain, these showers,
I stand for what is right.
Now it is time to retaliate those kingly kings-
With the blood for which they've stained.

O' with mighty strength,
I will strike with potent force,
With roars of wild thunder-
And the velocity of a bird.

O' with arm's length,
I have now slain the tyrant's core.
Oppression is all asunder,
And freedom is now ours, let it be heard!

"Children of Candy Rain"

Boys and girls of all ages,
Today is the day!
A day in rainy saccharine,

Into a bright path of new pages.
So tonight when ya'll lay,
Fabricate a rain, adjacent in-

The skies above that restrain us caged.
Now fly in love with every day,
But remember to candy rain our kin.

Continue the sweetness, and take stage-
To a world of your performance without delay,
And play this world as a violin-

Lost to rage;
Young children who's gone astray,
Keep the faith especially when-

The deadly come with war-fire engaged,
As their sights upon us dismay-
Our ideas, our thoughts, from within.

Now we must gauge
Of what is true and what is cliché.
And allow candy rain to sweeten our skin.

"Running-Man"

The Calm is in his storm-
As he sprints forever paced.
The blankets in his home-

Cannot shield his eyes in the mourn,
So he battles on, but not in place.
Is he running away from everything?
His eyes seem so supplied;
Does he cry the taste of ache in each pace-
So he could leave them to fall behind?

There's a distinction between this man and the rest,
His steps are of more echo with the world.
The silhouette of his body outlines the sun-fire-
That he holds upon his outward chest,
As he looks on with an anonymous secret curl.

What is he running from-
As he widens his stride more cynical?
His ambition is to never fall it seems,
Neither plunge into kingdom come,
So his legs keep pushing him on,
To lope on,
Especially when the journey is difficult.

When will he ever cease?
He runs bold with valiant endeavor-
Alongside his shadow, lighter than a feather,
As he runs on with inner peace.

Where is this man running?
Does he see the clouds structure-
Or sense the tempest coming?
On, he runs strong-
Without fear and without wonder.
On, he keeps running on
Despite the storm that which comes to plunder.

Why does he run in the rain?
Is it to hide his storm from within?
There is no denying-

That when it pours, he is the rain,
Just running down the sky akin to a lion.
On, he keeps moving on,
No matter the roar coming soon.
On, he keeps running on-
Amongst his solace of thunderous booms.

"In This Ink"

Where is the truth in death, but amongst the sighs?
The sighs there given brings us now to coincide-
With vivid remembrance of the soul's forgotten genocide;
Which now holds us plural to succumb the dreams of past's night.

The pigment of ones ink is cultured into care.
Captured by rapture, a once feeling never there;
Never here, nor never shared,
T'was the glory for us to turn unjust into fair.

And dying unto the might of silence
Bewilders the voice of joined alliance.
Now, as we stand proudly inked among those giants,
We can spend lesser nights alone and dying.

"I'm a Man"

Once in while,
A man has got to show no mercy.
So before I am taken,
I boldly stand up-
Tipping my hat,
Then I walk en-route to the perky.
Outnumbered three to one,

I don't care, I march on.
I then stand face to face,
Looking deep into their eyes-
With the silhouette of my pride,
And I tell them, "Go-ahead, just-try!"
"I am a man!" I told them.
So if you want to rattle this bush,
Then expect a few snakes.
If you shake the wrong one;
Go ahead and choose if you may,
Just be cautious to what bush you jangle,
Because in it may be where an anaconda lays.

"We Are the Judge"

The greatest of all the gifts-
Comes not in a box or a bow,
But more so an act!
An act of kindness which shifts-
All of ones kept sorrow,
So show simple compassion towards that.
One voice can make a difference,
Whether or not it is soft and low,
Or loud and stacked.
The only importance is giving,
Sharing, and caring,
So lay flat our arrogance and learn vivid temperance,
As for that is all we need!
When giving, we receive a seed;
That seed grows into beauty,
Thus, that beauty is a tree.
So it is our duty to seize each other-
And hold tight the roots of our sisters and brothers,
For our time is only borrowed.
Show simple love and claim no importance to hate,

Because through the judge of fate-
They may be gone tomorrow.

"Today in Tribulation"

Today, oh what a day!
I can't breathe and see-
The problems that befall my feet.

They send me gently on my way
Unto the day of my deathly-
Passage opens and rains colors to the streets.

I am so afraid,
With all of these problems that I see,
As they may well respire my heart beat,

And burn the day in shade,
Into a dark night of me.
I wipe the tears on my sleeve;

I notice no way,
Not a choice that I see.
I am just a man in need,

Of need of dreams to come today,
To surely see-
That I am not a waste, but only seen-

As a quiet voice, but now I want to say,
I want to be-
A smile of prominent dreams.

Still trying to find my way
In all these problems that I see.

Now I fall free from my feet-

To say,
"I am awaiting eagerly
The day that I am finally free."

"Confliction of Words"

My mouth won't open,
Although this ball-point pen still writes.
A fire thus emerges,
And combustion rains throughout the skies.

The blaze creates a reaction,
Allowing my eyes and heart to swell;
Then I feel the need to write,
As my heart befalls a persuasive spell.

I lose myself into time, space, and words,
An uncanny mindly syndrome.
Even though it seems as if phantasm,
I feel the joy within all of this delirium.

The fire walks up my skin,
So gently, it makes along its way.
It marches as if a band,
Coloring my body a much darker shade.

I am then black and white together mixed;
A fixed confliction of both neither skin.
I am thus no one,
And misconnected as the nether dim.

My eyes then begin to see,
Allowing me to be in tune with all the monsters.

I can either write away their feat,
Or rewrite a plot more fostered.

This war of words and reality-
Has taken control over me.
When that fire comes beating those warfare drums;
I only wish you too could see!

"The Traveling Quarter"

My name is George Washington;
The claimed father of the United States joined.
The plucky Colonial Commander to the Revolution,
And now I reside to the abutting of a coin.

I was minted into silver, the year of 1933,
For the man who had dreamed the American dream,
Bar for those years held the pits in American history;
We suffered a Great Depression, to which no one could ever see.

I first deployed into a truck, wrapped up tightly into a paper.
Annoying it was, but soon enough I was free;
Dispersed and let go to a bank without a danger,
Sitting adjacent to many others who looked just the same as me.

I was first given to a man in a flashy new suit,
As he cashed his first check of three O'nine twenty-five.
But pretty soon I became not of his loot,
As he in time had dropped me, and I rolled onward outside.

I sat in a crack in the concrete; I remained there for many days,
Until a boy then picked me up; his name was young Brian.
He placed me into his pocket, in the company of green grapes.
Oh such a pesky little kid, for the boy stayed steady crying.

Again I wasn't with this person for very long,
As I was now the decision for vanilla or chocolate.
In the ice cream parlor I sat, while listening to kiddy songs.
A few moments later, I was withdrawn from his pocket.

Again in a drawer I sat, but this time with a few new faces.
I was accompanied by some Jefferson's and a Roosevelt;
These two men seemed so pleasant and so gracious,
As they talked of many states now under one belt.

The most pleasant of all had to be my new friends, Abe Lincoln,
And also Sacagawea, for she was such a splendid lady.
I was so amazed of their dreams and all of their creations.
I just wish there was more time to hear what they were saying.

A boy then came in as the register was still open;
He looked very poor, very dirty, and very hungry.
The cashier then looked down to me as I was upright showing,
And he gave me to that boy so he could have a little money.

The boy held me gently as he was amazed by my shine.
He was in awe, as I saw a unique light within his eyes.
And I just wish, I just wish, that I was worth mine plus a dime;
For then he would've eaten, but instead he had died.

I laid in his hand a few days, and I just stared into his eyes;
All the things he could've done…
It wasn't my plan for young men to die!
Sad to say the dreams of men today is to attain me, Mr. George Washington.

"The Re-Public"

We the nation
Are deprived but surviving-
The tyrant with dedication.
But no more!
As for our eyes need rise-
To the government of size;
To rise up and flourish truth,
As within our roots-
We can overcome our own land,
And withstand-
The cost of living,
The cost of spending-
Without depending on bigger men;
And change the laws which drive us to sin,
Which govern us not men, but into poverty;
Because this is robbery-
From our own leading hierarchy.
So, we the nation need to stand-
And hold our stance, strongly demanding-
That we need to be-
Again a nation of freedom.

"Weaponry of Magnificence"

From what I can see
When out the door I step:
There are very little dreams,
So it means I must create them within my clefts.
My hands, these fingers, my voice,
They shall be the tools of wars ingenious choice.

The shadowed faces embark to find me,
To blind my see-full eyes,

Too yank out what makes me lively;
But I do not cry,
I simply make friends with my enemy,
Satisfying their hunger with artistic Amphetamine.

Dreamless, dreamless,
Come the retched awake,
I wait without cease!
Oh how I dare you, I dare for you to try and take-
My arty seasons,
That which make me so beautifully appeasing.

From what I can see,
Now, when I walk back up those steps,
There are so many more dreams.
So it means I have created a way within all my breath.
The eyes, my heart, the soul,
Is the artillery for the abiding aptitude I hold!

"Dream Killers"

Perilous eyes can steal *our* eyes
And consume the spirit in which we hold.
The dreams, plans, and our strategy then are gone;
What next happens is within the heart.
As they seed and drink out the soul, ceasing the creative flow,
It obliterates us into deeper woe.

They creep as they reap our deepest meanings.
Never do they die or ever fade;
And when I try to ignore it
They reappear and dissolve my core demeanor,
Leaving me a face that looks afraid,
Left troubled by living dreams next to their charade.

They're assassins in the slickest sense,
Scrounging around just like a rodent;
Taking not our breath but our childish smiles.
Then the day is gray until the end of time.
They're relentless in their torment,
Oh how their emotion is potent!

I feel the executioner getting closer;
To decease me, to kill my beautiful meaning.
Their smirk is sharp as the word, "Friends."
So deceitful they are,
This war is my defeating,
But now I shall render them!

I opened the doors of aftermath
And I dreamt there, where they never looked.
Now I am the killer to those dream killers,
So who ever shall stand against me,
(I'm speaking of those dreamless crooks.)
I say it loudly, "I will no longer brook!"

"I Am a Giant!"

This building in which I've built,
Stands strong, firm, and valiant.
I know of no other flaw, but guilt,
For I am a standing giant.
I've become the brick Masonic,
The builder of a fortified view;
Dreamlike, hence platonic-
To all who dreams lacking truth.
I am a standing giant-
In harmony amongst the skies;
The blue, the gold, and all the colors,
Which raise the soft-looked eyes.

The wind will not take me down,
Nor will any rebels!
I am fervent, thus sound,
Just silent amongst every level!
In all the crashing violence,
Other buildings are less than stark;
But I still stand so vibrant,
And sigh for those falling amidst the dark,
Because I *must* be that strongly giant
Who shall never fall apart!

"So Be It"

I will not die!
A man said I would;
Sixty seconds, a min-

Is all he said I had until I'd die,
Even though he said I should,
Because of all of my willful sins.

Should I die?
Even though I could;
However, I am not fond to the end,

So I will not die!
Shouting with the bluntness of wood,
In which I hold ready for them.

Now I, or them must die!
So I remained in place, I stood-
With my head high to those men.

I cried, "I will not die,
I am here to stay for good"

And suddenly then,

I did not die!
I lived, and they understood
That I will not die quietly today, amen!

"Merely Me"

The who I know I am, is all I know and see,
So what defines a man,
And what defines his dream?
Although it may seem-
In every way I can,
I cannot justify the means
To why I am the way I am;
I am just a man, merely me!

If who I know I am will later befall to me,
Then who is this man I am,
And why is he diverse from thee?
I'm not sure of what will be,
But nevertheless I will stand-
Adjacent next to me;
Even when I don't think I can,
Because I am a man, merely me!

If who I know I am becomes something not of free,
Am I defined as lost,
Am I but a dream?
Although it may seem-
That we all pay that cost,
We can never justify our means
For who had made us all;
I am just a man, merely me!

"What I leave Behind"

If I should die today or tomorrow,
I only wish for my gift to be given unto the world.
The art in it all has me envisioning fuzzy smoke,
Inside lies every boy and every girl reading
And singing of what I wrote.

Nothing truer in this life is as of death;
I know this because I have clarified it so many times
In so many sonnets, and inside vivid verses.
Many would say in cliché, that they just wanted forgiveness
For the hurting, either that they had lived by or based upon their past lives.

Not me!
I say this in complete self-reliance,
Because god and I have an understanding,
That the gift I had been given is to be beautiful in all forms;
"The passion in the poem I give, is my love,
And is where my heart was re-born."

Dying does not scare me,
I do not fear god and I am ready to be judged.
I do though fear the thoughts of my work never read,
To be locked away with me in a casket;
That, I could not indulge,

Even though I have denied love within my heart;
I bestowed it in a poem to live forever,
So I wouldn't have to fight.
This happens to be what I want,
This is not a statement stating:
I want to live forever; I only wish that for what I write.

What I'd leave behind is a pad of heart,
You will not find unfruitful paper.

Instead you will find a journey, the state of mind,
The essence of my life, versified and fruity,
Not prose; who's subsequent to an artist's beauty.

So if I should pass away in near time,
Please remember me and all I have dreamed.
From the journeys I have imagined as I shared it,
To the irrefutable passion read in every stanza;
I only ask to be remembered as a poet.

"Succumb to Corollary"

To die today, for me, would connote a life lived forever,
As dying tomorrow signifies death in norm.
A death a-morrow, yes, honorably I *will* be mourned;
Nevertheless, with passing time, the grand-coming of kin
Comes in with more kinfolk spawning in;
My name by then will had been forgotten and spent.
Conversely, with a death today,
It will open the eyes of those hearts as treasure chests.
So for me to no longer subsist the coming days,
My inner ink sonatas with the pen will be accredited forever-
Because I am promised to all the rest;
My name by then will have lived on,
Since I had died before my breath.

"War Carillon"

Chimes and rhymes tell all
As they strike the night of trust.
So be vigilant of tantrum calls
Unto thou fight comes abrupt.

It is sun-fall when war begins,
As the alliance of earth stands hushed.
In dire calls to man,
The carillon warns us of dusk.

"I Still Exist"

I was half past gone when I woke.
I awoke with my eyes to a room, a white ceiling
I noticed a starry type light;
Premature and dwindling before my time.
It wanted to pierce through the air and slice my ginger breath full-of life,
But I would not allow it!

Deep in contemplation I knew,
Death is in favor to the flower in the night
Nether the acceptance of light,
But not for me!
Death on this likely bed of takers
Is trying to take me without forewarning;
That is when I most loudly did so speak!

"Thou shall not pass-me-on into the night of sorrow,
Nor can thou blow out my fire with methodical winds."
On this eve, I shall possess breath again-
To light the candles of heaven to enfold my skin.

I shall then burn brilliantly over the shadows that follow me,
And more so past their predecessors-
So death cannot not follow me.
Death will then cease to sing its song.
I will not supply my spirit from my body,
Neither will I fall into my deep sleep untimely
Because I choose dwindle on!

"Blame me no More"

As I walk with eyes placed upon my back,
I share not a concern of wanting any more.
Too tired I have become in forgiveness which comes lacked;
I dare not ask for pardon just to suit the eyes adore.

The time for regrets is now left far past
Among the rest of fellow spoils;
Like a storm coming strong and with last,
It cleansed these shoulders, deep unto my soil.

So blame me not of what is gone now,
As I have done all I can to help and repair.
Blame me not, because I do not know how-
To keep taking blame for mistakes that once bared.

I am sorry for the pain in which you now blame-
Me, to which was not planned, however I am sorry for before.
But now I remain as the holder of same name,
Only for which to claim that you can blame me no more.

But if you cannot give absolve to all of the world,
I will repent no more, and walk proudly past
Carrying a smile to which holds one of curl;
I will then be blameless at last.

"To Die; the Pen or a Gun"

One breath at a time, I witness these crimes
Which leaves us the choice:
Pick up a pen or a gun,
The minimal choice; write rhymes or die under the sun.

These days are getting harder;

Mothers and fathers are crying every day
With not an ounce of hope to comfort their weary souls,
Leaving pain to scratch out God, the only hope in which they know.

These coming days I plan to die,
Die without retribution, but charismatically;
Therefore, I plan tonight,
I will live forever through all I write.

A pen or a gun became my option.
I've held that fortified before,
But the pen is lighter and holds more force-
Then that destruction of life, the coward's choice!

So if I die, it will be by pen,
Because in all I am, I am just a guy-
Who holds crumpled paper within these hands;
I am a poet, I am a man!

-The Color Black- Act II

Black is the beauty of the night, but reflects the pain behind the eyes…

"My Sweet Lily"

There was a dream that I dreamed-
Last night in my sleep.
I thought I was awake,
Because, Lily was with me.
My heart jumped and it rolled,
I could not control-
The upshot of it all;
Of my sweet Lily annulled.

What I seen was so sheen;
Her scarlet inner flowing's-
That which were in attendance on my sleeves-
Was yet outer flowing-
Onto my hands.

I bellowed to the heavens,
"I command you Lord"
(Yelling for her vengeance.)
"In the name of my Lily,
Come now, come forth,
Bring back my sweet Lily!"

I cried and I wept,
In a sleep without sleep;
I could never forget
When she left-
And she slept-
Her eternal dream sleep.

I tried to arouse
And wake my sweet bee,
Who was so dry without her honey.
Though it was proclaimed her time to sleep,
I could not let her go,
Let her go in peace.

I ascended her body up,
(She was firm at full length.)
Still crying cherry rain,
I asked for her forgiveness,
For not being more a shielding man-
In this world,
For she was fruit to lesser hands.

I then arose from my sleep,
So anxious, so worried.
And as several tears had fallen from my cheek,
I then felt hand in hand with my Lily,
Which defused my hearts increase.
(Oh the beauty of my Lily!)
I then held her so close,
Never to let go my sweet Lily.

"The Onset of Forty Winks"

I awoke with shoes within my vista;
Many colors, many sets, and many sizes.
I could not stir up any more strength,
For just one fleeting look will so then decide me.

I am only able to look straight forward,
Onward, forever intermittently-
Into the dark, light, and all in between;
Flanked by a rascal beside me and soiled debris.

The suns venture was vague,
Although I reluctantly had to take more than forty winks.
The repast is the stink, so whispered,
(If only he did not eat that or have that last drink.)

My thoughts were of interior and exterior,

Although I was by now beside of my heart.
Gathering also my viscera;
I thought, what now could I possibly impart?

Yet, so still the tone was,
How I felt various judgments gawping upon me;
Such bliss can be felt from them-
As they wait and look-on, and decide to stay its conclusion with glee.

I feel as if a dull fish,
One which is yet left swimming in concrete cherries.
Only to be left to the superiority over ice;
To think of warmth is too contrary.

After long, still one pair there stayed;
The color, the shape, and its size-
Were at rest, awaiting my final scarlet swill of breath
As I subsided in the will of those eyes watching me die.

"Butterfly to a Fly"

I watched a butterfly turn black.
The only light left was inside of its eyes.
Then that too was then consumed-
And attacked,
Turning a butterfly into a fly.

I unlooked-for its change.
But its seems the larva had grown from within-
And gave thousands of compounded eyes-
In exchange;
In trade for that butterfly's vibrant skin.

It then cleaned its wings,

For the stench of death surrounded it whole.
That aroma gave it pleasure;
Such a disgustful thing-
For it to wash, clean, and patrol-
Like a grungy king.

A butterfly to a fly,
That holds only now an eerie buzz.
The attractive wings are now decayed,
But spry;
It is like that butterfly never really was.

"Imitations of Life"

Can I live?
I feel the urge to breathe-
When I plead the fifth,
To protect what I cannot see,
Which is a replicated me-
Acting on what not is.

Am I truly alive-
If alls I do is reproduce-
White lies within these eyes?
To only deprive my heart of truth,
What then am I of use-
If I am disguised and feel obliged to lie?

My truth is not the exact,
But more so, just a guess.
You can call me a flippant of an act-
Who leans more towards what looks best;
Only to mask how I address-
My own quandary of the facts.

To pretend is my command.
I eat and exhale a masqueraded truth;
This is the sham-
That I cannot let loose-
Or refuse,
Because an imitation is all I really am.

"The Contrast Peephole"

Late the night,
And so immature my sleep was,
That I had forgotten to secure the latch-
Which besat my doors clasp.

Silent neon moon-
And translucent life flickered the windows-
In the replication of fiendish ordinance-
Among me as I walked-to.

I secured the lock-
Which was assembled to my door;
And as I turned around,
It reassembled, becoming no more.

The door itself too,
It all diminished into nothing.
A dream above a dream so outlandish,
Leaving left a scope to look in.

There was total blackness,
And left was not me, but only a hole;
The peeping kind, which seemed to me,
It wanted me to look in and see what be shown.

From a mere stride away,

It looked to me as a pinhole in the darkness-
Just shining a string of light-
So bright, into the unending night.

I then put my eye to the peeping hole,
Although its presence was doorless without pair.
I then looked into a white room-
In which no colors had yet been there;
Only pure pallid floors, walls, and a vibrant moon within that room.

There was no way in;
No doorway into that light so bright it seemed,
Only a peer into a reality not beseated for my dreams.
Thus, there is only darkness for me.

"The Last Piece of Chocolate"

In the milky taste of sorrow,
Tonight, I embodied its every stoke.
In all the nights we shared and borrowed,
You chose tonight to leave a note.

The kind of words you chose to say-
Left me in all of disarray;
When you explained you could not stay,
For another heart holds your ship at bay.

Left in the dark by russet candles,
I now sip this wine alone in my closet;
With left imprints from your sandals,
I remain with a ring left by chocolate.

"Margaret Joy"

A joy for so many, whose heart was plenty,
My darling, my love,
The penny dropped, a penny;
I knew I had loved my beloved-
And no other,
Oh, how I loved my Sweet Jenny.

Many years we enjoyed,
And had I not thought-
Nor could I imagine it'd be destroyed,
So on and on I had fought-
This secret, this love-
That I had for Margaret Joy.

But with this love I trice had,
My sweet Jenny, my sweet Jenny-
Grew more and more sad,
For she thought she wasn't plenty.
She thought I had forgotten,
But O' words, O' nothing did I add.

So, too I got sad;
In the middle of the night,
I grabbed some stationary, some pad,
Thus, I began to write, oh how I did write;
Blaming my sweet Jenny-
For something asinine as I got mad.

I explained with such annoy,
How I loved her no more.
I said, my love, there is another I enjoy,
My heart for another does adore.
She is more beautiful than you;
Postscript, I love Margaret Joy!

So there I bared shame,
A-left to her bed,
So she would wake and lay claim-
To all the sordid things I had said;
My love for Margaret joy,
Thus, how it became.

And devoid of no a' morrow,
I walked beyond our still home-
With lone tears to come tomorrow,
To a woman I had left all alone-
With a letter and a reason,
Because it was lust I had followed.

The next came a' morn,
Such a morning I enjoyed,
For now I tell who I adorned,
I told my Margaret Joy-
I loved her-
And no one else anymore.

She said she was flattered,
But she had yet another lover;
And with her eyelashes, she batted,
Turning around to her other;
Forgetting *I* was there,
Leaving me left over chatter.

I then thought of Sweet Jenny,
How she'd wake, she would wake-
In seconds, just any!
Then on my way, I did make-
Back to our home,
And back to my Sweet Jenny.

I rushed with winded bust-
Through the streets and the crowd,

Faster than a gust,
When I felt my sweet Jenny screaming all aloud!
I ran faster and faster-
When I felt my heart come unjust.

As I rushed through the door,
Standing there was not Jenny;
Her footing was so high above the floor,
Without life, without any;
All of her breath had been spent,
No more life, no more Jenny…

"Angel in the Beast"

A tattered man, a beast,
Resides in denied beseech-
About his need and plead for love-
High upon his bastion, that is stationed in the clouds so loftily above.

A beast in need of love;
Such a pain unbearable without the calming of his dove.
To the beast, he requests no guests,
As too quick he gets sick and attests,
"He wants naught else but relapse with a spouse that lays to rest."

The stars amongst is where he gazes,
Since on earth his dear grace has dated-
Far long past, for which had passed a while ago;
Such pity this beast has not released from his soul.

The thunder is his placate plate,
For it too rages with ire, immense flashes of pain and hate-
Towards a world that curls our smiles unevenly so;

In a way which sways a man into a beast unto the much greater woe!

The keratin in his blood grew much richer,
Stemming out jagged nails as like a twister;
Curling out to bring closer no one,
Only more wretched for darkness to bare no sun.

His visage bred a much fuller coat,
And with time, his tone rasped mourning within his throat.
Never again will he resemble a man,
As long his bosoms flam amasses imprinted marks of his long-left Suzanne.

"Tit for a Tat"

A tit for a tat,
The get back in which holds no slack.
Where this was that, and was be that;
The game is played among whist knacks.

A tit for a tat,
The joy of splendor in which be mapped
For the eyes do pleasures of sweet get back,
keeps thou rendered within lost black.

A tit for a tat,
A come back, in which strikes back;
The sweetened tender as they lay flat-
Holds one to remember of bitter payback.

"Too Beautiful for Me"

This feeling, this dream,
That I see and I feel-
Makes the beauty in my theme-
All the more real.
With a touch to my face,
I aim to embrace-
The beauty of my scheme,
Which seems so surreal.

So I dream what I feel,
And I feel what I see,
But where is the real-
In all of my scheme?
With my face out of touch,
Do I seek so much?
I'm starting to infer that this is the theme;
Dreams are just too beautiful for me.

"Aren't I Pretty?"

She was a little, not so cute little girl-
Who spoke in riddles; who tried so hard, young lass.
She stuttered, and she muttered-
While the other kids jointly laughed.

She tried so very hard-
For her voice not to break apart, not to shake.
They all mimicked her, saying cruel words;
Calling her ugly, while pushing her around by a lake.
Day after day,
They came and they came, never did they miss their mark.
Way back when, it was winter then,
When the sun fell sooner, so it was very dark.

Still they all teased,
As their faces looked pleased, such a shame, such a shame.
So without any remorse, it was just like before;
Except the darkness this time had messed up their aim.

Into the lake she then fell,
Where she yelped and yelled so loud
For someone to come, and it be done;
Rescuing her from that icy hell shroud.

But no one would come,
For it was done; her death was widely spread.
She died with hate and before it was too late,
She vowed to come back and claim those kid's dead.

So as those kids lay,
She comes out to play, singing a soothing ditty.
So when they awake, she rises from that lake,
Singing to them all, "Aren't I pretty, aren't I pretty!?"

She claimed them one by one
With the song she sung, she had no pity.
Soon those kids were all gone, now left be that song,
"Aren't I pretty, aren't I pretty!?"

"Effigy"

Stranger than strange,
He's looking at me with those eyes.
I can't take it today!
To intrude he seems obliged,
But I am not,
I want him to perish, now die!

Yet another day, he stays,

Swaying me unto I think deranged.
He stares at me,
He gawks, oh how it is driving me insane.
Look away,
Before I can no longer be blamed!

This day, it is my turn to stare.
I look uneasy into his silent soul;
He stares back,
No remorse, his temperance ever shows!
His eyes are black,
Dark as the ness of coal!

Equally, we forever stood,
As my eyes upon him patiently stayed
For fear he'd strike when I turned.
But that day-
And those hours never became;
For it was just a statue, hence, dead I lay!

"The Stay Stair-Man"

There is a man atop my stairs
And I see him everywhere;
He is there every day!
He also rests aside my bed,
Standing and staring, as my dreams dream away.
When I bathe,
His image dampens my mushy skin.
He is the reflection when I shave,
He is my pockets ball of lint.
The man atop my stairs is there,
His figure resembles my blackest dreams.
He is there,
Can you not see!

He is there, I undoubtedly scream,
"Why, oh why have you come to visit me?"
And he just stares,
Looking deeper inside of me;
Is he there?
Or am I falling into insanity!?
He also lays' above my ceiling,
As it is there he catches all my dreams;
He steals the ones which are appealing,
And feeds me back the ones too mean.
He is still there, can you not see?
I am afraid!
He is standing right beside of me,
I just wish this man would go away!

"The Patriarch of Time"

The silent creeper, who holds not a peep;
A swindler of seasons, a cloaked master thief.
With no one to appease him, he knows not of grief,
Be it his reason for leading us into old heap.

With the stroke of his hands, he alters youthful faces-
Into old bland, wrinkled beyond something tasteless.
And before you can hint it, he steals you into nameless.
Like a night rapes the day of the light of its placing.

He then leaves you alone and shivering in the cold,
While claiming all of whom you know;
A fiend who never shows,
Rendering you naive to the fact that you are aging old.

"Remembrance"

The clothing, the perfume, and my hand,
Will itself not another day;
For it is lost and carried into gone,
Shedding a moment of nothings fade,-
Oh how wrong!
Where pebbles forget as the times of sand-

Breathes soar it's wishing memories.
Frail, oh how frail one can be-
To a hoped figment of no one there;
A no one to no longer see,
Who now not stands next to me.

"Paradise Lost"

Too long at sea, so where is thee?
Upon tasting greed, where dare I go?
Into nights or unto dreams?
Though I seem seized,
Indeed I don't know.

Too far from home, is there another?
I am alone, so am I still here-
Walking the path of wonder?
I seem to be sundered-
By a tone of thunder and sultry tears.

Too far-fetched it sounds, but can I grasp now?
I am bound, so I ask please?
And upon that I ask how-
Can I attain Utopian clouds?
But it was renowned; Utopia, you can never seize!

"Silk"

Once a dream, now fathomed into creation-
Through your body of silky coated tender;
I lay to rest my eyes in dirt forever enslaved in-
A beautiful death that I wish befalls me into splendor.
Came the night, whence a shady fisherman sat.
He told me of death, along with its holder's name.
Though he seemed uncanny sitting there with his hat,
I was open with all ears, amidst the thud of rain.

His lingo was eerie, oh how he warned me of silk;
A death so smooth, with no way to be captured.
It vexed me how blunt he was, that kind of ilk;
I am odious of his insolence, now I want to feel the rapture.

I returned the next night, sly as a cat in the dark.
There again he sat, alone with a cigarette.
I crept, and I crept, as he smiled of my lark;
As I thought of his death, wanting to hear his regrets.

Holding a blade within my sleeve, I grip it firmly strong.
Held high, now I, only I want to feel his life slowly wilt.
Quick, oh how quick he then turned, his blade had killed me gone.
He then whispered in my ear, "Your death was smooth as silk."

"Loveless Endeavors"

All the time, past hence visits the uneasy psyche,
The basis in which makes thee untidy among thy spirit.
Nice or mean-
I cannot go forth without knowing thy merit,

For thy kiss upon my cheek seems like a delightful goodbye.
But not a soul can determine if or how the heart feels,

Nor if it's dire resistance to let one go tonight,
For I know not anymore what thy zeal appeals.

I'm diminishing into a ness of dark-
And I cannot see the light.
Whence I stood has become ones quirk,
And transformed my smile to thy upside delight.

Thou rendered me feeble and unable-
Among each spoil, even to a needles prick.
A silly notion for me to fix myself into stable;
As now being duped has left me very sick.

Hence, the motive to conclude those finer thoughts,
And now become a fixed pessimist of love.
Contentment has not a face anymore, for I sought-
With all of my might; now I am too taken thereof.

"For who is Not There"

In a time of prime, I chose myself to give;
My soul, my eyes, to a far dream that never is.
For who is not there, I have no one to assist,
As my time here on earth became not one of bliss.

I perceive sound as a lonesome wishing man,
In whose hope that wishes for a distant view of land.
Oh to I, I know not why or where I stand,
For who is not there comes a flagrant taste of bland.

Their presence never became; a who never shared.
A game for which it claimed; a soul held despaired.
Quick, so quick the who's turned into ware,
Changing all one knows into who was never there.

"God Astray"

When I gaze at the sky sometimes, I'm not sure what is there.
The clouds, the sun, the stars, the moon,
All amidst each-other in air;
Sitting… without the presence of you.

The way I see it, you are there at times,
But sometimes I feel without help,
Without faith, only held to crimes;
In the rasp of my vocals, for you I yell!

Devoid of where you are,
Am I just fine without the attendance of your face?
I don't feel so by far,
And so my heart for you is in a never-ending chase.

Going the distance of existence is something I will do,
Just to get a hint of who sits atop the heavens.
What I am most afraid of, is if there really is a you,
Then I will understand who I pray to every night around eleven.

I search and I search the clouds for your trail;
Although, never do I find a trace of the gracious you.
I know it's odd to search for something, even though I know I'd Fail,
But I don't know what else I could do.

"Ill in Love"

I've got this pain deep within my bones;
A pain of forever sick.
It is setting fire to my veins in rush,
Causing ruby images of blush-
In a romance not one of pick;
I am restrained to what not I own.

My thoughts have me seeing sane,
Whence I cry, no not I!
Becoming the insanity of ones abyss-
Holds onto a bandage of not my fix;
I ask why-
Do I shy here in sicknesses claim?

Like the open hand is without a cleft;
I am an empty land lacking facet.
Tied to loves neglect,
I hold onto with all my best-
My sickness entrenched in drastic,
Consuming all till naught be left.

"Not Enough"

When can it ever be so?
A dream I dream coming out of hiding?
A dream that I dream who never hears no,
Rescuing me from my books damaged bindings.

I seem to have lost my way,
And I step not an honest step into the night
Because I am darkness within my fade;
A shadowed mans never enough in the brightest of lights.

When withered as a flower, I dress to remain silent;
For who I shall be, gives an excused face,
Only for the moment when seemed most vibrant.
I then blossom fear, in which its roots hold me in place.

When I count the vacant stars in the sea,
I count the dreams never fulfilled, but once wished.
When I see the star that I desired for me to be,
I drown within sorrow, holding onto my own abyss.

Freedom was never meant for me,
I am just embodied by dreams never spoken.
Once a time I believed, so I fought and I dreamed,
But in the end, I was left absent among the broken.

I waited and yet waited for a silence to become vacant,
But at last I figured a dream is only meant for sleep.
I never again want to dream and see me make it;
I only wish to not walk nor take another leap.

I break in stillness of a journey never taken.
Oh how silly I was to think of this crazy stuff.
I dream no longer, as my eyes begin-in fading,
And now I see that I was just never enough.

"Scars of Rain"

Draw down those shades today,
I feel like sleeping in.
My heart does not feel well this day,
So I say,
I wish to adjoin this pillow along my skin.

The sunlight is just too much to bear,
So I darken those windows of mine with black paper.
With commemoration of no one now there,
I supply a tear to never share,
And abandon the thoughts which no one has catered.

The phone has been ringing off the hook;
It is family, to see if I am okay.
But everywhere I look,
The pain is still as thievery as a crook,
So I hold my head lower down as I lay.

The days for me no longer have light,
As I always wake a quarter past ten.
I try to sleep right,
But what is true about the night-
When alls I can dream about is back then?

I am exhausted from being tired,
And so weary of just trying.
If only I could suspire-
A new meaning which means higher,
I wouldn't feel like I am slowly dying.

Now it is raining,
And I can hear the thumping upon my roof.
So along with my pain-
I can too play a symphony upon my windowpane,
As I see ravage lightning somewhat shining through.

I walked out that door
And let the rain slide down my cheek.
It was pouring to my adore,
So I prayed for a whole lot more,
To take away what has made my heart very weak.

I stepped amidst the thunder outside,
Away from that tainted roomful of memories-
Where we once lain side by side,
And for so long I have cried;
I feel it's about time I wash away the you left inside of me.

"The Lion and the Fisherman"

Among the view of wretched plains,
There had laid a starving lion.
And be it not for his hungerish eyes,

He would have never thought twice about dying,
As his stomach was growling-
Louder than all of the other lions.

Though he sought and sometimes he claimed,
His hunger maimed for more and more,
For a meal that would satisfy.
A bite or more he adored-
Became his quest of life;
As then his journey led him to foreign shores.

It was there he hunted just minor fish-
Seasoned in plankton spices.
His eyes appeared more and more human,
For his hungerish wild-side no longer sufficed;
Leaving him more serene and understanding
Of the phase he was in, the seasons trice.

He learned to adapt to his famine,
Becoming the smartest of all the beasts.
While lying one day on the sandy shores,
He noticed an animal walking upright on two feet;
He stood tall and lengthy,
As his language to the lion seemed far a leap.

The lion approached this animal;
The closer he would get, the more he heard in pieces.
So be it not right by law,
He had forgotten that he was more dominant species.
So he spoke to this animal;
How it looked so amazed in the lion's keenness.

"I am fisherman!" the strange animal had said.
"Where do you come from?" He asked-
With no intentions to get a reply.
But the lion had replied in a mass-
Of words so clear;

The fisherman's smile was so vast.

The fisherman then came to say,
"How do you come to speak?
This is an awkward side to things."
The lion just said so meek,
"I am just undone by foods so wild,
Maybe that's how I came to feat"

"Well then," the fisherman had said,
"Come to my side and stand.
I am Fisherman, that's my name
Like I said, a man!
I catch these yummy fish on a string;
A simple task with so less demand."

"I catch them too," the lion had stated,
"But my way brings lesser food.
I use to eat bloodier things…"
"Hold it Lion! I don't mean to be rude,
But I am among those things you ate,
I am not sure if you knew."

The lion said, "I have never seen your kind before,
So don't be wary of my looks"
The fisherman looked convinced enough,
Not worrying of what he had read in all the books.
So he continued talking to the lion on fishing;
A skill he explained done with crooks.

The lion had tasted blood before, but never he thought-
Of how men tasted, so it never became trend.
As the fisherman began to think,
He had no reason to fend
Or be scared;
The fisherman had then accepted him.

They walked for many hours
And shared each other's reasons-
For being,
As their relationship had lasted for many wonderful seasons.
Suddenly then, the tides began to decrease,
While increasing more their wilder demeaning.

There was no more fish to their shores,
And the lion looked more and more hungry.
Then he thought of his friend, the Fisherman,
And saw him as food of different sundry.
But he thought, No! He is my friend,
And the lion laughed while grabbing his tummy.
It was then he guffawed,
While rolling on the ground with pride.
The lion then felt a quick spike to his ribs,
Causing him to widen his lion eyes.
It was the fisherman with a spear,
He was lying in disguise; the real lion, the lion had realized.

"The Man Under the Streetlight"

There is a man outside my window;
He stands under the street light, silhouetted.
He wears a dark hat and a trench-coat;
His face is blurry, as his shoes look of shredded.

Each night I see him,
He's wary in his looking ways.
As his eyes burn a matched dim,
His coat sways in the breeze of May.

Each season that brought new weather;
Clad in black, he remained unchanged.
Bringing only chills devoid of better,

I just hope he knows not my name.

"All the Write Reasons"

To whom this may concern,

I say "whom" because I don't know you;
I am speaking to you, Love…
Where there has been pain, you never gave praise to me,
You just let me be.
Even when I was most afraid,
You never desired the days-
To stand strong right next to me.

Just go away,
I don't want you now!
Single-handedly I faced the rain,
And now I have been swayed-
By the frameless walls and empty sheets of melancholy.

No memoirs of past loves-
Since there was never one to talk about;
No stories of worship or reference to loving songs,
Only common language, because the word "love" was too native in tongue.

When I called out to you, Love,
I was left alone…
When I prayed for you're arms to hold me,
None had held me tighter than that of my own.
I thought something was wrong with me…

For so long I was disheartened-
By the fact of knowing no one loved me,
Not even you…

Prior to the desertion,
I had readied a room for you in my heart;
So exceptional, it was beautiful,
And I knew, I knew, I knew
If you'd ever show, you'd never go.

After all this time,
Now you have come to release me?
I don't see why,
But in rejection, Love, did you know-
That with passing time you've become my enemy?
I cannot open my heart to you,
I don't know how, and I don't know why,
But I am okay with that;
So just let me be and set me free-
For the right reasons that you, Love, had lacked.

For all the wrong reasons, Love,
You think I would still want you after all of this.
No! I will not give in to you, I insist-
You just collect your baggage from my shelves,
Because I like it better by myself.

"Bitter Bread"

Sometimes when I'm all alone,
I think of all the wrong that has been done.
The tears that I have tasted-
And wasted-
Leave saline within my bones.
I'm so bitter now because she is gone!
A silhouette of depicted images is what I see;
(Her imprint is still present in my bed right next to me.)
And left on a silver spoon is her lipstick.
The last I seen her, the moonlight had sat upon her hips.

The next morning she was gone, so I awaited her return;
Though she did not come home, nor did she pick up that phone,
I just imagined, by now, she was feeling quite alone.
But that was not the case, because the next thing I knew,
My red heart had begun to turn a bluish hue.
I am so bitter now,
And I know exactly why;
The breaded-heart I had for her was complete with butter,
But she wanted margarine, who was yet her other.

"X's and O's"

I was born an X, but made of O's.
So when will I fit-
And match this shape I hold?

There have been many, I must say!
So should I try to match them-
Or scarcely stay away?

Some say, I am unique;
I'm not sure why, but my question is-
Why don't I hold X's or O's physique?

I do not fit with X,
Because my mind is said to be too wide,
And I do not bear a cross along my chest.

I also do not fit with O,
For reasons I can't oblige;
Maybe it is the fact that I am not at all enclosed.

So if I am not an O,
Or even an X,
I have to ask, where do I go?

"Sometimes I Cry"

I wake up every morning and I look to my right;
You are no longer there,
And I feel so contrite-
Within all of my heart; that sight, I can no longer bear!

You're indention is still upon my bed,
And your scent… I swear is still there!
I can't make you leave my head,
For everything reminds me when you were once here.

When I look to the mirror,
I see you standing right there,
And I have to wipe the image clearer-
Just to make you disappear.

Every shirt I have worn, I shared it once with you;
So what am I supposed to wear-
When it has been worn by you too?
Please fill them back up and just reappear!

The nights are getting longer.
(By that, I mean restless!)
Even though I can be stronger,
I choose not to and remain awake breathless.

Why, oh why has this begun to ensue?
I just wish I'd not remember-
The fiery things you do;
Your blaze left me a bitter ember.

My heart has gone astray!
Why, why, oh why-
Are you the one who remained okay,
And I was left lone to cry?

"Where Have I Gone?"

This feeling I've been getting lately-
Has me thinking insanely.
I feel I am somewhat missing,
"But I am here!" so says that mirror.
It's not as if a puzzle piece is lost,
Instead, I think it was never included.
I can't breathe; at times it's hard to catch my breath.
I feel arrested within my emotions, so I am secluded.
The direness of this situation is so scary to me-
Because I am here, but I feel somewhat gone, you see?
Wishful thinking thinks I will find myself one day soon,-
But where have I gone?
I am a spider without a web, who only assumes,
Assuming that I can create a bridge over to myself.
I cannot put my finger on it,
I attest that I am gone!
I will testify to a judge that I don't know where I am,
And I don't know where I belong!
Where did I go!?
I don't know who or what has taken me;
Am I the captive to someone I know,
Or is the captor only me!?

"Broken Hearted"

It is a sad thing when you cannot smile-
When one thousand trials find you innocent,
But still you are desolate.
It has been a while, but the pain just won't subside,
When the presence of the moon compels you to cry;
As a matter of fact, it is everything.
Anything and all, even the smallest ling-
Can remind us of the love we once held.

(Oh, how it hurts to hear those wedding bells!)
Tonight,
On this night,
I feel it so much deeper,
And I cannot stand for one more dawn,
Because if I go on, I will fall,
And nobody will sing more a gracious song than you.
I can no longer hear your siren calls,
So I paint myself up a saddened blue.
I cannot see your face anymore,
It seems you have vanished along with my heart.
So I cry to you, I scream, I implore,
"Come back to me before it gets dark!"
My heart is painfully aching,
I feel it slowly de-rooted.
Oh how could I be taken-
When all's I wanted was your soothing?
I am fading, because for you I long.
I'm fading, I'm fading!
I am de-shaded,
I'm gone!

"Ripple of Darkness"

The ripple of an empty room
Is now of sweet savor
To my soul, my demons,
Which hold bladed sabers,
Awaiting so patient
For the light to diminish;
For being in darkness
Lets hell roam free in it.

"Moments Ago"

A moment ago, love was not here,
It was not yet embedded.
A moment ago I loved,
Even though I never said it.
A moment ago I prayed-
For someone to arise and a withstand-
The moments not long ago that held me swayed-
With ache; corpulent with the pain of a declining man.
A moment ago I found you,
So beautiful and yet so pure.
A moment ago I lost you,
Now all's that's left is imagery of former blur.
A moment ago I smiled,
Because you were my dividing line-
To the moments that long ago took,
Giving me back the life I had far left behind.
A moment ago was just here,
So how can I get it back?
It seems the moments of long ago has prevailed,
Cunning me to think of nothing but that.

"The Abyss of Self"

The night is late,
The phone is at a halt.
Neither woman nor a face;
Just crystal darkness upon my cot.

The walls are placid white,
Though the shadow so covers it all.
Questions that used to come light
Are now heavier, so now I fall.

Into the night I wondered off,
Into the shadows and the worry.
I had walked so dreamless up-to my loft,
And it was there I began to scurry.

Madness had befell my grin,
I could not think nor could I reason.
The only thing I could picture was then,
As I lost touch with the current season.

Winter then became these walls;
A bitter-cold barrage had surrounded my bed.
Summer then emerged in thrall,
And melted the ice so beyond my head.

The melt had become a river,
My bed had learned to drift.
I am now to be delivered,
I am now controlled by the darkest grips.

Fingers overwhelmed my skin,
Crawling my body in comfortable woe.
The shadows then played a violin,
Taking away my most-inner glow.

The darkness has come, so I surrender!
The light has forsaken me without a truth.
The last comfort I can now remember,
Was when I became the darkness, a shadow too!

-The Color Red- Act III

Finding comfort in the darkened shade, the starry colors of night begins to shine with love…

"A Night-Spent of Poetry"

How about we do something different tonight?
This may sound a bit unusual,
But I would like to talk poetry with you, will that be okay?
The usual conversations are fine,
So please don't think that they aren't;
I just wish to express myself more to you through annunciation,
But by doing so, I wish to express it in art.

So this day, this night, it shall be all about poetry.
Me and you shall rhyme and free verse our souls,
So when I say I love you, just know…
That those words come from the deepest element within me.
I only wish to become closer to you-
In hopes of conveying our relationship even higher.

I desire to hear everything you have to say.
Just to prove that, tonight, I'll let you choose:
Speak on your regrets or your bluish blues,
Or maybe the color of your stylish shoes;
Whatever it is, I am all open!

Tell me your fears through verse, don't be hesitant;
And I shall rhyme back is absolute assonance.
Tell me the love you hold deep inside your inner mind;
Because by doing that,
We shall be seen as the sublime aristocrats of love.

The understanding of you is all I want.
To know what, when, or how you feel before you feel it.
I wish to feel it all too and cry for you before you begin to speak it.
So tonight, let us speak straightforward without silly pride
And side the complex words which hold little meaning.

I only wish to speak with you in poetry,
Because any other way to say I love you, I feel is overrated…

I feel it is spoken too fluently.

"Beauty by Recipe"

To construct one of beauty, you first need to dream;
Dream of a flower, and then soak it in some rain.
Now color it with sparkles
And twine it in with inner marvel,
Topping it off with sprinkles of sour pain.

Next, you blend the dish, while wishing a selfless wish,
But be sure to season it with brackish tears.
Now stir carefully as a witch,
Tasting between every few whips,
Just to ensure the cleverness in which the recipe holds dear.

Lastly, place it in the oven and wait about an hour,
While you remain for the smell that holds perfect expressions.
Then comes the scent of black roasted flowers,
So now bring out this dish of ours
To savor beautiful imperfections.

"Of Many Dinners"

From our window I looked in;
Looking into the window, our home.
I was ready to walk inside, until when-
I had seen that inside, you were readying for us to be alone.

You were setting down the table place,
Placing a setting for just us two.
With such amazing grace,
The gracefully amazing I seen was in you.

With new deep brown china on the table,
The brown seemed much deeper within your eyes.
Oh, how your beauty appeared present but fable,
Your presence was yet more beautiful than I had ever surmised.

In the window I still looked,
This window of ours that holds you in;
I seen you tapping your foot while cooking,
While tapping the beater to the hips of your apron.

Such an incredible thing it is,
How I know something such as, "love" is credible-
When I look at you positioned there, preparing all of this,
Preparing and positioning, so carefully, everything that is edible.

You next looked for approval to the mirror,
Turning the mirror for modest approval the way you do.
After so many of these endearing years,
My dear, I am still so in love with only you.

You were then lighting those red occasion candles next to some warm bread.
You had that red lipstick on, the one the light shined off of.
I then acted sincere walking in; that is when you smiled, and said,
You said while I was walking in, "Happy anniversary my love!"

"Out-of Our Virtues"

I like you, you like me too.
Nothing more this night could be named-
Other than, "innocent."

You're scared, I'm scared too.
I can't believe this moment is here-
And I'm spending it with you....

Your first time, my first time;
The delay has been luxury to our hearts-
As they are now mended as one in aching passion,
United and fastened all-together as one part.

This is innocence…
Pure as the waters of Norway.
Your eyes, my eyes;
They are set upon each other in deep calm
Awaiting the breakthrough of our virtues.

The horizon…
It is winding down, given a marigold blush upon our skin.
It's as if a river of immaculate beauty has risen-
Amid your velvet kisses and my abrasive touch,
While we make subtle passage into faultless such.

All the while that illustrious inferno has falling,
Leaving just a moon to surround me and you,
Along with a barrage of stars in longing,
Giving highlight to this moment they never knew.

The sky is circling around us,
Giving the nights our deflowered love-
With sun-fire of lustrous bust,
Till the days go by with bye.

To die inside comes words expressed so shy,
But we shall never lose-
That avowal in each other's eyes which said,
"You love me, and I love you!"

"A Note Within A Poem"

I don't discern how to say this…
Losing you will be my conclusion, and-
Overly my soul will wilt.
Velocity will then hobble me, and-
Effuse my sorrowed guilt.

You did not deserve this…
Overall, I reflect what I have done.
Understand that I am sorry;

Always remember me for the sweeter songs I've sung!
Lay away the past, and-
Will yourself to love me again.
Always keep in mind the clever things I've embellished, so-
Yomp past the burden in which I've given, and-
Suspire the secret message!

"Donna Red"

I knew a girl back in my younger days;
She smiled of sunrays,
She was distinguished as flawless.
The kernel within her eyes showed such brilliance,
It's as if she knew it,
But her modesty was exuberant.

Her marble skin radiated such a force;
She was more than her inner more,
I felt she was beyond it.
This night, I reminisce on that sweet girl-
As I lay upon my bed;
Oh how I remember that picturesque Donna Red.

"Wedding Vows"

The bells are ringing this afternoon.
The sun is shining, and the birds are performing.
The hour is awaiting our matrimony this June,-
And so am I!
To wake this morning for me was hard for me to come to,
But deep inside me, I knew-
That you would be waiting for me at that alter.
I have to say that I am scared to unite our eyes,
But as long as it is with you, I can manage,
And no other man shall love you more than I!
The afflictions you have taken away from me has saved me,
So this day I will marry you,
And our union will be so graceful.
But just before I put this halo on that finger,
I wish to say thank you!
The love I have come to know is so different,
As it is splendid.
I feel the distinction between you and the others,
So I could never imagine that second before I met you;
Only the minute after, when I became amended!
Your face was just so perfectly imperfect,
And with your grace as an angel,
I fell in a tangle of love that instant.
I just knew, so I do!
My darling, I do…

"Secret Diary Entry: In Love with a Friend"

One day, I hope with all hope-
That I can be the one she loves and sees.
I would wish my three wishes-
All the same wish without end, without cease.

If I could dream the same dreams,
I'd pick the ones to which we share.
If only I'd wake and reawake-
Just to see her presence lying there.

The prayers that I pray are indeed all around,
But in every "amen" I do say,
I say,
Dear lord, let her see the picture my heart portrays?

My emotions are so passionate;
I feel so lost within this love.
My desire for her eyes have grown so much-
To where she is all I now think of.

The half-truth is not the whole truth,
And because I love her, I am divided-
Between affection and a friend, who does not seem to notice,
So I have to try to hide it!

"Mother of Pearls"

Come all, O dreaming minds,
Into the land of eternal shine.
Where reveries are awake,
And your beauty is guaranteed
Because that splendor comes innate.

The dreams, O that you have,
Supply shade for what's left half
In a world so empty full.
Like a cup of buoyant knack,
You are cosseted in gift-full wool.

So keep pace, my sweet babies,

Continue to turn those tired pages.
For this is your fate
And purpose of your strength;
To create ingenious places.

"Hiatus Smile"

I remember a time,
Not that long far-past it seems;
I was anxious and sedated with hatred,
Only to find out that the only person I hated was me.
"Dearest Lord!" I called out.
(I asked an imaginary query.)
"Why am I alone?" I asked with a quiet tone.
There was no answer,
Nor a guided direction out of the state of falling weary.
I then fell asleep amid the doubt in my heart.
When I woke, some time had passed;
I was a bit older and did not know it,
But the brown of summer leaves outside my window had been lapsed.
My dwelling had seemed a bit different;
It seemed to hold a feminine touch!
I sat up and sipped from my bedside cup,
Not realizing that before there was no such.
I took notice to a picture within a frame;
Me and a beautiful stranger were standing side by side.
I felt really anxious,
Especially when I heard what seemed to be a cry.
I walked out that room, following that strange sound.
Behind this wood door is where it seemed to be.
I opened the door, and there sat a lady with a baby,
And that baby resembled like me!
That woman stared at me with such love;
It's as if she had known me for quite a while.

I then remembered that question I had asked God,
He must have heard me;
Putting me in hiatus until I could smile!

"Love Me Back!"

Away, away, away!
Whether love is fiction or fact,
Your return has been a blessing.
So today my dear, love me back.

Today, today, today!
Just be there when I open these eyes;
Be frail, and care-
If you may, and shed an ounce of pride.

Be gentle, be there-
To show me there is still life.
Be sweet,
And be caring, just as a loving wife.

Be there, be there,
In all my trials and errors.
Ward me in danger and love me,
Just care, and hold me in your mirrors;

Those eyes, your eyes,
Which don't see me in all I lack.
So tonight, this night,
Don't lie when you love me back!

"Spell... Father"

Ask me what a father is!
Many words hold many meanings,
But there is only one word which holds the same;
As its opposite is accredited by definition.
This word is special in its bringing-
And deserves recognition!

Ask me of its definition!
The strong, the righteous,
Who is always there when needed.
The provider, the protector,
Who shall never leave, but instead just-
Teaches and provides safe sector.

Now, ask me how to spell father!
You will think I am erroneous
And incapable of signifying it accurate,
But still my answer would be the same,
And I will sing it harmonious;
Spell father; M-O-T-H-E-R!

"A Nameless Kiss"

Her touch to me is simple,
Being of none can compare in logic.
It brings my hair to stand much stiffer,
As my every follicle looks to want it.

Her face is of depicted pigments,
Forming the right place for all her features.
Her smile constructs of dreamed figments,
Creating a faultless splendid creature.

Her eyes are deepened with teases,
A well of watered beauty.
And they contain me without all reason,
As they drown me, oh so smoothly.

But I cannot explain her kisses;
For there aren't any expressions.
And if I could have but one of any wishes,
It would be to understand those brim dimensions.

"Stranger Love"

I once kissed heaven;
It was a marvelous thing.
Except I was left only guessing,
Holding a heart which then forever sang.
How it happened is kind of odd,
Even though I have no complaints,
For she had blindly robbed-
My lips, lacking the knowledge of her name.
You see, I had to catch this train;
It was heading for downtown,
Then she appeared a bit faint;
As then I came around-
To catch this falling angel-like saint.
She then rewarded me with a knightly kiss,
With a sudden smile into my soul.
I felt of pure bliss-
From this beauty I did not know.
She just walked onto the train
As I stood there and let her go;
I never got her name,
And indeed I miss her so.

"A Breath of Fresh Err"

My darling…
Your love has given me the breath I've never held,
One which my chest has never felt;
The feeling of my heart fully stark-
Without the blatant "-ness" after dark.
Only dark eyes- that which can hide a coin
Within those fountains of drizzled beauty.
You had given me life with just one kiss,
And so on… with yet another.
When you are by me, I am free,
And so on… until you leave.
Then the world is all in weary.
That is when I miss you the most,
When I am nothing more than solitary.
When you're here, I can breathe-
As you stand close next to me.
However, when you're gone, that air you easily gave
Is so easily taken away.

"Ready to Love"

Love… oh love,
Why do you hurt so good?
Love…
So in love,
I am not sure if I should.

Love… dearest love,
How could I resist your charms?
Love…
I'm in love, so in love…
With the thought of you within these arms.
Love… sweet tender love,

What is the distance between us two?
Love… I haven't had enough,
Because I'm in love…
With only you.

Love… oh my love,
Will you now shine as my light?
Oh love…
My sweet love…
Surrender to me come tonight.

"Family Matters"

Family…
In the word alone, it stands strong and long.
And in it is me standing along our once wrongs.
But together we overcome, and we remain strong.
My family; a unit, a bond no hand could ever draw.

Family…
Alone we never are, as together we fight joined.
We are all different in our ways, as of two sides to a coin,
But still the same body of matter connected, never coy.
We are adhesive in our love, as of the moon is made of joy.

Family…
Oh how sweet it is to look inside our kingdom;
Just a minute is needed in this family's freedom.
If I never knew them, then I wish one day I'd meet them,
Because nothing compares to my family, except if you were dreaming.

"Keeping the Faith"

Where there be rain, there comes thunder-
Striking the calm sky fixed on trouble,
While it tears all to sunder;
The heavens will not easily go subtle

Deep from fire unto water,
The desire blazes a fascination;
Never again, so why bother?
Twill misery be but loyal destination?

The gloom shall make dire residence;
Claiming you, is what it seems.
But having faith without the hesitance,
That is the dream devoid of needs.

"Little Innocence"

The easiest thing you could do is walk away;
To walk past those eyes who adore you so.
The tricky part arrives when you decide to stay,
Since a further shadow follows you on the go.

They know no better of this world;
You can call them the purest thing.
From their eyes, a boy or a girl,
They rapidly become your hearts loving pain.

When they smile for no possible reason,
It is such splendor to see their eyes rise.
The way they look at you when you greet them-
Is beautiful enough a reason to just die.

To them, you are the faultless hero;

A super someone, with the greatest power.
To them, you are not a zero,
And they will still love you among all the hours.

You are their air in which they breathe.
They console the mood in which you take.
Be gentle of a child's needs;
A child's innocence, you sure can't make.

"Madness in Love"

Long since this feeling be felt touched my stay heart,
But once again it has found a way.
It runs through my veins as a raging rivers start,
And leaves one with no words; nothing more one could say.

How can I resist the urge of love when it is pleasant?
Or more so, who can ever taste so sweet?
In dire song, oh how the heart gives presence,
Breaching the shelter to where love and pain greet.

One thousand trials may find me guilty,
But never let I go.
Whence loves insanity bares futility,
I remain by love and never let I go.

"Midnight Keystrokes"

I once met this girl, a sweet girl of tender;
It was a long time ago, but I do so remember.
It was midnight; coming the presence of November,
But already snowing as if the month of cold December

I was walking a path that I had many times before,
And there she stood gazing afar, I just couldn't ignore-
The beauty that came with twinkled eyes only for mine to endure.
I knew right then that love at first sight would open its doors.

I stood beside her, silent, but still she looked on.
A painting of creation she was, like the setting of the sun.
I tried to speak, but yet my words came to none,
And my presence remained quiet standing next to my one.

She stared on without hesitance; never once did she see,
A man in love, a man in need, a man that which was me.
She then turned away slowly, as if waiting for thee,
But I couldn't give eyes; I couldn't even breathe-

As I watched her away, I felt my heart skip a beat.
I wanted to yell and scream, "Please come back to me!"
I then mustered all my courage running hastily down the street,
Now… she is my bride to be, oh how sweet.

"To Steal an Angel"

There is no better delight
Then the stars of one's sky.
Indeed with ardor tonight,
I ask not to fight-
The lure of her angel eyes;
For tonight I thieve away her breath
By a tale of not a lie,
And I will give her console, for just lest-
She holds not more of heavens delight.

I want not one thing more
Then the brimming of her love.
She is the entirety of my sights adore,

So I just couldn't ignore-
My care for this angel above.
So when she wanted to stay,
I reached my arms extent because thereof.
Because I did, her angelic light had shined away;
Leaving her human, now present upon my door.

"When Mom Smiles"

I know not of many things,
As this world gives plenty terror.
For who is nor top or crop of the cream,
My mother has changed dark haze into better.

Among all of the given tests,
I presume that I have somewhat failed.
But as she joins me on each given quest,
I can hold my head high, without sigh, with proud sails.

When the time comes of wearied state,
And the clock strikes pain from troubled dials,
I just look over to her face,
Then all fades away, when I see moms smile.

"A Day for the Lord"

It is about the time I prayed.
So I say this to you my lord,
"Take me when my eyes shut close,
Not tomorrow, but now, today!"
Even though my thoughts dismay-
The common sense I should have,
Especially when trouble rushes in as a horde.

The bountiful love you give is all I need,
It is all I want!
(I must be gracious in your memory)
From Adam and Eve,
I am your extended seed,
And I can feel your presence within my bones;
It is like you're speaking vibrant life inside of me.

I am full of hope because I can speak with you.
You are the question and my answers-
That lies within my vapors skin;
You are the sense in the common clue,
And there may be not much I can do,
Nevertheless, I will try;
Furthermore, Lord.... this day I give to you!

"Love, Wings, and Such Things"

She awoke with the birds
Among a sunrise-
And spoke with soft spoken words,
And I realized-
She was all I'd ever need.

The flowers came to bloom,
And there we both lay
For many hours in our room,
Until the day had taken shade,
As then in came our dreams.

The clock by our bed-
Spun all around,
Circling its tocks over our head
And down to the ground;
The exact time was never seized.

Her eyes were untold,
And I could've just died-
From the flecks of brown and the gold
That was there in her eyes;
It had brought me to my knees!

The spell I then held
Was so much and so more,
As then I swelled and propelled-
So much higher than before;
More superior then the trees.

I then felt so much joy
Looking down at my world,
As upward I deployed,
Then downward I twirled,
Gliding on a gentle breeze.

And as I do fall,
And shall I come down,
The world will heed my call-
As I undoubtedly renowned,
"I love you, Louise!"

"The Homeland of Lost Children"

Brothers and sisters, come proclaim your throne.
Three paces ago you were lost,
But now you are home.
So taste the zealous froth of family,
As your smiles which are dandy come no longer alone.

Lost children roaming these lands,
Come all forth, there is plenty of room!
Take grab to your neighbors' hand,

Now hold on,
And be calm as the tides of sand.

Your time is now little ones, so be strong!
You dreamt for this day to arrive,
For wishes to just belong.
It is of no matter where you're from;
So welcome all lost children, chant your native tongue.

"Let Us Dance"
(A Tribute to Michael Jackson)

Tap, tap, tap,
Our feet retract in remembrance.
On the moon we walk
Without gravity, without hesitance.
In the clouds we stand,
We remember, we dance!

Let us dance away the night
And embrace the morning skies.
Let us spin around the town
And light up these lights, our eyes.
Let us dance,
Let us breathe and eat surprise.

Tonight we play that beat,
That beat which greets you right.
Let's make rhythmic feet to fly-
And soar to sweet delight.
Let us dance,
Let us speak, "I want to love tonight!"

Since that one day we're here
Seeing life in all romance.

Next moment, we are gone!
So, stomp your feet, clap your hands all the way to France,
And love one another;
Let us dance!

"Evermore My Love"

Time is no longer of the essence,
For our love will outlast all the sunsets.
Our best bet-
Would be to just pray and hold on-
For a more gracious day to spawn.
Now is not the time my love to be scared,
It will all be okay in still time,
As our love is a never-ending hourglass of prime.
We are a flame of precious crimson,
A voice to all lovers' indifference.
Our alignment is of the stars-
When we adjoin both our hands
And demand-
More time for worship.
That is when we must take it!
Eternity is the resting place for our hearts,
So my love, there is no hurry,
Don't worry,
Our time is adorned as evermore!

"Eight Roses"

Sometimes it is hard to give away roses;
I suppose it is kind-
Or decent to give away such a precious thing.
It saddens my heart though-

When those roses are mine,
But then become another ones gift less -ling.
It is but just a flower, I say;
Don't cry for those dear red beauties,
With pedaled lips of prickled stems.
So give away those eight red roses today,
Especially to those who need them.
Away, away!
Send them on their way,
Until there are no more red doses.
Away, away!
Spread the joy of eight roses today.

"Unborn Child of Mine"

Her smile will be one thousand miles;
I can't believe how perfect she will be.
If I counted my blessings, it would take a while,
Just because how she would make me feel.

Her eyes would be such a prize;
That glint will be one of a kind.
It'll be as if I've reached my high,
And I'm flying among the heavens.

When she puckers sweetened lips,
I'd feel such a lively feeling within.
When I'd hold her upon my hips,
That little girl will look at me so recognizably.

Her little hands will remind me of my own,
And her grip shall be mighty strong!
She is the love I have not yet known;
My unborn lift to a higher elation.

Her very being is just my dream;
A creation of who she will be.
She is for yet not seen;
Oh, this unborn child of mine.

"Crispy Tongue"

Roses and dandelions;
That is all I could find my love!
Is that enough or shall I bring more?
All together it counts four;
Would that suffice my darling, my dove?

I also found a box of chocolates;
Do you covet something sweet?
Will neat milky elegance be sufficient,
Will it adjacent our distance?
The menu is all you please.

Hugs and coos;
It is all for you, if you desire.
My voice is soft attire for your mind
As I whisper sublime.
I'll exalt your eyes ever higher.

How about the moon?
You'll have it soon, I promise!
The solace will be found in all I give,
And is-
The best way I know how to present my fondness.

How about me?
I am free, so can I assist?
Merely a kiss is my only bid,
But it will surely light you heart lit.

Besides, my heart is the last gift there is.

"When you're Asleep"

Tonight under that gorgeous moon,
I watch you beat that round thing by a mile.
The beauty that you maintain when you're asleep
Is even more a reason for me to stay my smile.

The way that moonlight hits your hips
And the way it shadows your earlobes;
I cannot explain it all better than this:
Your beauty is unending with the majestic flow.

I wish you could sleep in that beauty forever,
Only to keep my heart as warm as it is right now.
The loving things which were never meant for me
Seems to care more for me today somehow.

I have to say, I have never felt this way before;
It is both comforting and a joy
Because I know when you're asleep,
My constant staring of you will be embraced, not ignored.

My hand upon your hand;
How good you feel and how warm those fingers are!
This is the feeling I wish the world could know,
The feeling to be imperfectly marred.

That ring around your finger is still there I see,
And our love still stands so very strong.
There have been many years that you've spent next to me,
And each day you keep reappearing in the sunrise, so our love can go on!

The simple sleep you hold is beautiful,
Especially those later sleeps till noon.
And with each wake, I know you would always declare to me the same,
"My darling, I love you!"

"Eyes of Invariable Change"

The spec in your eyes has always given me hope.
They shine of apples, not cut in slices,
More rather, always full in form.
They do not judge me or fault me unfairly,
Neither will they shut-close to forget about me.
Instead, those eyes of yours had stayed with me all this time;
That just goes to tell me that your eyes are mine.
They've reflected and held my secrets, fears, and my smiles,
And had given me back the happiness I had forgotten when my eyes fell wild.
There is nothing more cultivating than your eyes right now-
As they look upon me like a king.
Your eyes under the night sky-
Shines, and gives me more meaning than I could ever have dreamed.
And though it seems your eyes are out of place;
Like they should be amongst other stars in the night
Or with the crescent moon because your eyes shine so bright;
Your eyes do not wonder off and stray far away from me,
They're always open and always with grace.

"Lovely"

What do I call you?
You are just so unreal.

Your presence fills my heart.
So what do I call you?
I certainly do love you,
And I don't know what else to feel;
Unsure of where to start.

How did it come to be,
For you to become so lovable?
You are my beautiful experience;
The most precious I have ever seen.
Your eyes seem so gleam
In a world so unsuitable-
To your soft, little eyed glance.

You are so heavenly,
And you are so beautiful.
You are my inspiration,
And you hold my hearts key;
Unlocking all of me,
And without doing it so cruel
You allow my hearts expansion.

You take a big part of me
And you fill it with parts of you.
You hold a smile that is bubbly,
And completely I can see
That you are entirely a part of me,
Like the sky is made of blue;
You are just so lovely.

"The Love Flower"

When we speak, it is an undemanding aim,
And as we seek, we journey through noticed change.
Who we are is simple, but no less than words,

Under the truth of our skin rests our beauty being stirred.

When we find that feeling of stormy bliss,
We craze their style, their demeanor, and their kiss.
Just is the fact of minor pleasure, to subside tickled butterflies.
We need, we want, and we dream of nothing but their eyes.

When we talk, we emphasize the idea not yet created;
Of love and happiness, or for so whom shall sedate us.
But love in hiatus is rather a flower yet bloomed,
Weary not, as the flower of love shall be absolute soon.

-The Color Purple- Act IV

The mix of the cosmos enables you to mastermind and create the magic that is hidden…

"Surrounded by Words!"

I once read a poem,
It seemed to me so nice.
The words were slick and flowing,
The cuts to the stanza were sharp as a knife.
I thought, I too, would like to create something so astounding.
So I wrote and I wrote,
But nothing came close;
I felt the presence of nothing inside me.
I looked to my left and I looked to my right,
But I could not grasp the idea of how, or what I should write.

So I read that poem again and again,
But this time, I had seen a flash of a bearded grey man.
I began to think, that he was the link;
This is who makes those writers eternal in their think!
So I prayed and I prayed,
To god or who may,
May so grant me with the grandest of words.
But when I picked up that pen and nothing came from,
I began to think, this was absurd!

So one night, out of many that I've had,
I decided to ask-
That bearded grey man for many words to be bestowed upon my mind.
I just wanted to dress my vernacular richer
To claim a name the world would forever recognize.
The next morning I woke,
I choked and I chocked;
Many words were inward left and right!
I coughed and I coughed,
The words wouldn't get off;
So I picked up a pen, thus, I began to write!

There were so many words with so many feelings,

So many thoughts,
I just could not believe it!
Such wily skill and beauty sublimed;
I began to see the world in all of a rhyme.
But then I got tired, so I thought I'd retire,
Except those words wouldn't let me;
They kept me frightened with words such as, "Fire."
And If I tried to escape, they did not have to chase-
Because when I thought of being captured,
I was then in a cage!
I am going insane,
But I am all who to blame;
Now I am the one who is read by many others.
The words don't stop to rest,
Now neither do I,
Because I could not invest-
Nor take the time to practice my rhymes!
Although these words are astounding,
They're draining me whole;
Still, I feel so consoled-
To these words that which now surround me!

"A Magnificent Hunt"

It was the era of shadow,
The sun was right for this day.
The shades were sharp and narrow,
Now like my arrows.
It's of the moment, my turn to fade.

I look to the sky for the time.
I look to a sun which is no longer there.
I see the night pour like dark wine-
Without fine shine;
The only sparkle is of my sweat, which tastes the air.

My feet are standing by for the right signs;
I dare not move unto the wake of thy prey.
I wait, and I wait for the time
As my skins salt declines;
I wait for it to break for the coming day.
I can smell it in the winds.
I can see its glowing eyes.
I am not feeble, nor sad to its frowned chin,
But merely humored to its ruse it sends;
I will swoop in with all disguise.

I am the pasture for which it roams.
I am the soil in all the ground.
I linger among the winds monotone;
I am not natures clone,
More-rather the echo in its sound.

I am the silhouette that stole the night.
I am the outline of all that's dark.
Wherever I step sheds not of light,
But of my unlit delight,
For my hunters strike will make thy prey depart.

The kill is now mine to take.
I am standing by for its witnessing eyes.
I wait, and I wait for its sip to the lake,
As I too am bathing away, I fake;
Now thy prey, it is time to die!

"Awaiting a Storm"

When a silent evening brings new pain,
I look to the sky at night
And I await the rain-
To place my frown upside tonight,

To coat my pain;
And maybe, just maybe that rain
Will finally give me delight.

So I wait;
I remain still and silent
For my fate
To wash away the residing,
Of which resides in me, innate;
The pain, the tears, which sate
The wretched tyrant inside.

It is dark outside, but I remain.
It is quiet and ominous, but I still stand,
Awaiting the rain,
So I can be cleansed and wrought into a man.
So I wait away my pain,
And it may seem insane,
But I refuse to be damned.

So, I wait for the sky-
To open up and swallow my body's might
With ravish force, which deems me survived
In this world of lies, that I now fight.
I will leave not an ounce deprived,
And my skin will shine beaded glints of disguise;
Transforming me into a man, through rain-drops come tonight.

With thunder, with lighting, with rain, and with more;
I open my arms to the ferocious winds
And I soar-
Standing still, while tears rests my hind,
There is nothing else I would adore
Than rain-falls pouring, cleansing my marred core;
Leaving the pain from the mind.

So rain on me,

And release an ocean upon my head.
Rain on me-
And leave nothing else to be said.
Rain on me,
And take the ache from me;
To everlastingly sleep in rain and claim it my bed.

"Boat to Paradise"

I once visited a lake, a ways far outside of town.
It was modestly quaint with the silence of birds.
So I desired a stroll with the company of no words,
With not a quandary to be heard, nor not even to be found.

I walked with the echo of hush, and not a soul had seen me.
I just walked, and I walked, until the suns inferno depleted.
As the stars then breached, I found that my defense was no longer needed
As my worries disappeared like the sun under mere knees.

While then walking, I came onto the sight of a boathouse,
And I then followed my eyes until they met its placing.
I was cautious, but able in facing-
The mysteries I had felt, which held my mind aroused.

I walked around the beams, massaging softly the wooded grain.
I then placed my nose to the dead timber, absorbing its strong scent.
It reminded me of change, and how the past could be bent,
To make peace, after a time once left in wane.

I glanced within the boathouse to find a tattered white boat.
It was dressed with dirty rimming, and the path before it looked diverse from mine.
I then lifted a foot and carefully sat inside,
While looking down to my feet, I noticed an etched note.

"Look unto the heavens for serenity, and not the boat."
I knew not where the boat would take me, nor how I would get myself back,
But I just thought for some reason, this boat would lead me beyond the sky black;
So I then closed my eyes, as I unfastened the boat from the pier.

I then felt a little sickly, my stomach felt unstable.
I wanted to leave quickly, and as I opened up my eyes,
The light was so unbearable, that it readied me to cry;
My eyes were yet unbending and no longer even able.
As my vision started to clear, I could see a snake-like river course,
And it was leading into the sky, held high by golden gates.
But sure enough I had the patience; I had no quarry for the wait,
So I could feel the light of all lights go deep within my source.

The boat though was in no way a fast pacer,
As it glided and shifted from the left to the right.
A day then day had passed, carrying me unto the night,
As now I am swayed by hunger, the last and only danger.

I stood up from my seat, jumping head into the water,
And as I dove under, everything seemed very clean.
It felt to me as a sleep, filled with velvet dreams;
Once I dared to blink, it all dissolved and it altered.

I then found myself falling amidst many clouds;
I was declining so fast, I couldn't hear myself yell.
I couldn't even tell-
Because the sonic boom was so very loud.

Shooting like a star closer towards the slowly vessel,
I had made up my mind to die and never want to know.
But as I came nearer to my end, my body began to slow;
Leaving me once again onboard softly, untouched, and nestled.

So I waited again, and again, trekking the days in dire hunger.

I knew this place would take me, so I ought to last it out.
I knew this place was special, and not once did I doubt-
That what was on the other side could ever leave me sundered.

I went on for a week, slowly making the days.
Hungry; so hungry I was, as I fell to my weary knees.
Then while looking up at the light, I came to my final means;
I could no longer carry on, I never crossed the gates.

"Cloudy Schemes and Water Dreams"

Frequently I-
Have been dreaming of clouds,
So I-
Feel as though a cloud,
Darkened among the shroud of night.
So tonight,
Within all of my sight,
I will weep clear dye
And thunder to the world aloud.

I feel this storm brewing inside me,
And I see it's never ending.
Oh 'gee,-
How these thunder-bolts are fending
The storm of all the trespassers;
My keepers,
Who scorch this night ever deeper.
I am to be-
A wave of dreams pending.

Hovering above all these men and women,
I love it!
Especially baby children,
To see their eyes when I drip,

Raindrops resting on their skin, the sensation,
Forming condensation;
Their faces, the wide-eyed reaction!
So I send-
Endless water to emit.

I will rain the world of my beauty,
And immerse this place-
In my duty.
Touching every face,
Molding their dreams,
So I scheme-
Aqua love to their needs,
Leaving flecks of fire sooty;
Then gone without a trace.

"Continuation of Psychosis Labyrinth"

I came across an old man;
He owned a white beard and a stick.
Upon rain slaps on tin cans,
His tone hollowed a raspy, but happy wick.
He was awaiting a spark to ignite him,
To tell his muddles of pick,
And envision the whims inside him;
He seemed more so to me a man that was rather sick.

There was confusion within his eyes,
But to an extent, a certain truth.
His ways endued his eyes
To be more soundly, lost within his boots.
Thump, thump, thump!
He asked me why I wore that suit;
In which question had given me goose bumps,
As he then suddenly yanked out his tooth.

With that incisor he disturbingly pulled out,
He then threw it up in the rain.
How it elated him into a Laughlin sprout
Vexed me into his own derange;
The keenness to his Ritz,
As he put on an act of insane.
A maze lost within his wits,
It sure was a delightful fane!

He then amusingly snapped his fingers,
Snap, snap, snap!
So for a while longer, I lingered;
Still listening to these tin cans rain slap.
I was enticed to the beauty he saw,
That I couldn't see past;
I had neither insanity nor duality to fall-
Deeper into a spiral; a lunacy nap.

He then said, "Come here young one,
I have something to tell."
"I am not crazy, I am just having fun!"
But then he suddenly fell,
Causing crimson madness to poor the concrete streets.
His head was dampened with what felt-
Like a cherry dream; a leech-
Which dragged me into his mind of dreamer's hell.

T'was a madness ambling me into dementia.
I felt as a kite flying the water beaded sky,
As I lifted my arms highly, going nowhere, still amongst the vista.
I then noticed my clothing was quite very dry.
The tin cans still slapped,
Causing a rhythmic fortified-
Relapse, where now bluish rain retracts.
To further stay, I seemed much obliged.

The starry night seemed a great deal of quiet,
As the rain paused in all its rap.
Nothing seemed unsafe or violent
In the presence of all that was that.
The panorama seemed upside down
And was bunched with stairs and traps;
A world deformed, but sound,
Hither, amid my thumping taps.

A stranger then came amongst me in silence;
He was painted with stripes of bluish red.
His conduct seemed funny and violet,
So I laughed loudly, cracking my tooth, and in pain I said,
"Why do you wear that suit?"
In which was formerly said.
And then I had yanked out my tooth;
Pretty soon, I too had cherries flow from my head.

"Dreamland"

Silent tonight,
So what indeed I do?
I am quiet, but now I plight
To change the world for me and you.
As I write…
The nature in all things seems just ripe,
For now it whispers to me as coo.

Listening tonight,
So how dare I dream?
I am calm as the striped persistent white-
Lines, for which run the street.
I fight-
Purely for the right-
To breathe, in this humanity not so neat.

Speaking tonight,
So how should my accent be?
I have listened with might,
In the silence of dreamlike schemes.
Splendid to say with delight,
I am speaking tonight
Of the beauty in all I see.

Dreaming tonight,
So will I transcend extreme?
I am sleeping just right,
Subdued in a web of lineal supreme.
I feel no longer contrite-
For leaving this night-
For a night of undying dreams.

"Into the Night"

The day is simple,
Although the night is mysterious within shade;
I took a walk one day-
For example,
Into the dying light of a forest so immense;
It was more than ample.
This woodland I speak of danced,
And pointed me the way to a hushed serene glade.

It was there that I thought the night was splendid
And all most perfect,
But there was a flaw in it all, a peculiar object.
My feet wandered to where my eyes had planted,
And I knelt upon my knees to see-
That this flaw candidly-
Resembled me;
Triggering my heart beat to erect.

I was clothed in a dirty cowl,
And I tried to open my eyes;
But it appears I had already died-
To the sound of those nightly owls.
There have been odder things, I must say;
In my dreams, I avow!
But I am awake this very day,
Sending myself off to nightly skies.

"Dream Catcher"

For some reason lately,
My dreams just won't sleep.
I can feel it so greatly,
This feeling, this moment, and my needs;
To flicker, thus succeed-
For a higher meaning maybe!

I cannot describe it,
For these feelings have no words,
But yet I am subsided-
Within beauty, and the possibilities of all of this earth;
I'm not sure.
(I feel so, so, so lively!)

Some days when I lay though,
I dream vivid vibrance.
I can't sleep a wink, I clearly know-
That my dreams are at their finest.
(Oh, how they're shining!)
This day, this hour, they more so do glow.

So, instead of an ornament lain above my ceiling,
It is me…
Just catching, not stealing-

The dreamiest of my reveries,
So I can clearly be-
All of which I'm dreaming!

"The Water Elemental"

I can imagine this, and I can imagine that.
I can imagine me imagining myself right back.
I can do anything, and I can feel everyone.
I have been in sync, with rivers, oceans, and the sun.
I am everywhere!
I am the flood which sees no end,
And I can disappear-
My body, which may be composed immense.
I can feel everything, and I can clean it pure.
I can also sing,
If I sang away all of the earth!
I can create new life; hence, I can taketh away.
I can also trick the light
And sparkle it in vibrant ways.
I can take away ones breath,
Or I quench ones thirsty mouth.
I will be all that is left-
If this world continues this loveless drought!

"A Symphony of Ghosts"

Chimes and bells, oh my!
Music, melody, and harmony.
This world feels pleasant tonight,
And I feel in all accord-
With the wind of which so quite.
Ding-dongs and ring-a-lings tune nice-

Along with my feet's beat and fingers snap.
A magical musical trice-
Has visited this day, as I slap in tune my lap;
Whack, whack, whack!
Piano keys strike, it feels all just right;
The only thing missing seems to be a drum.
So I looked all about and found me a bucket;
Next sound to come out was, bar rump-a-bum-bump!
The saxophone was then singing,
And the violin was in full woe.
The mixture between them both-
Had easily enamored my hair coned.
Each tuneful apparatus had its way with any ear;
And as it appears, they're ghosts, who are playing all alone.

"Annexed Reflections"

When I appear in the mirror,
I glimpse sheer magnificence.
With flaws and all I appear-
So perfect, but defectively engineered-
Into my own quintessence.

The touch to that glass window-
Has altered me abstractly.
This fellow is now mellow-
As the blush of soft yellow,
While it depicts these eyes so cautiously.

The coldness of that reflection is no longer there,
But in its place, my warmth has transferred.
The kindling of my heart is flare,
As my fingers sparked me unaware-
Of being transmuted into that mirror.

"The Orchestrator"

T'was a summer afternoon with not a care among the earth;
There was this static of emotion filling up the atmosphere.
And be it in no doubt known, I knew not what to assert
Of this energy I felt brewing, nor why it was here.

It occurred to me while walking in the park that I always had,
There was nobody to be seen, not a soul was around.
While the trees, the wind, and the sun wore their known clad,
My skin abruptly converted to the pigment of dark brown.

I then suddenly felt the need to jump and to play
Among my fellow trees, who had grown and developed.
I could hear them all whispering, speaking of the month after May;
How there was so much rain, that it could fill a skies cup.

I stood still with anxiousness, feeling kind of weird
As I listened, and just listened, I wanted to hear more.
I then looked to my hands and a long branch just appeared;
As I felt really tall, so much higher than before.

Within a few seconds time, I was as high as the trees,
Claiming the vast sky and all its pretty blue.
I felt much more alive and much more so free,
That I started to cry leaves, leaving left very few.

I felt somewhat cold and naked, as if not wearing any clothing;
So I reached further to the warm sky, then I-
Started to feel more tepid, and without even knowing,
I began to grow more leaves from deep within side.

I then ambled past my brothers and sisters, and as I walked
They all gawked, talking in murmur.
It seemed as if I was changing simple law into naught,
And as I marched on, my branches grew much more so firmer.

I next shouted to the sun with a tree voice, as I grew;
"Take me into beauty, and take me into dreams!"
I then disregarded all I once knew,
Leaving left my creation of for beautiful schemes.

I then danced with the wind as the leaves created ease,
And with my tree body, I bloomed scores of fruit.
I then wisped up butterflies, and then I seized-
The entire world, while orchestrating a choir of my roots.

With ready arms, I then pointed to the north shores,
And I grabbed all the ocean.
Bringing water as I roared,
I then bestowed it into motion.

From my presence, which be south,
I looked to the west and then to the east;
While holding out my arms, I shouted from my mouth,
"Let me now feel the dark breeze!"

I then clapped my hands together, and in came the night
With the abyss of dark far.
I then threw up my arms with all of ones might,
Setting fire to the sky, while instructing brilliant stars.

With the wild ocean still waiting for my demands,
I softly laid it down, forming many rivers.
And as I stilled it all smooth with my tree-like hands,
I shared the glee with fellow trees, which were joyful in mirth.

When I figured I was through creating this place of no name,
I observed all the land and I noticed no color.
So I then whooshed in a cloud that held abundant rain,
And I sprayed the entire world to the essence of myrrh.

A few minutes then passed with delight now in the air,
After the mist had desiccated, leaving behind signs of its glint.

I then looked to all the plush and I dropped lone a tear,
And as it struck ground, everything became a hued tint.

I can now look upon it all; my so beautiful land,
As I rest with all awe in the comfort of none.
I had changed human law without bounds to these hands;
Next I enjoy, since finally I'm done!

"The Magician"

Unraveled from my sleep one night,
I fell into a sleepless wake.
I awoke with my eyes wide open,
Journeying down a path I did not take.

I wondered around for a while,
Only to stop by a massive oak.
This tree was very colorful and rich;
It all seemed to me a blandish joke.

I was not there,
But there I was so lively and alive.
I was not enlightened one bit,
Only amused and surprised.

I began to hear some hullabaloo;
Someone was excited it seemed!
I looked all around,
But there was no one there but me.

"Who is there!?"
I so profoundly shouted.
(I thought, maybe I should speak a little louder.)
"Come out, come out you cowardly coward!"

No one replied back,
But there were sparks of neon flashes;
It was coming from behind the oak,
Bright lights emitted in back of it.

I then walked behind that great big oak,
And there, someone very small had stood;
This person looked very old,
Plus he wore a tattered bluish suede hood.

He was waving what looked like a twig,
But why was it glowing I thought?
It produced such beautiful colors,
As he waved it and picked up a rock.

He jumped so high with glee,
Oh how he seemed to be so happy.
I heard him shout some odd words,
"Shaplacky, Shaplacky!"

Dropping that rock,
He then fixed his eyes upon a small pond;
He swung that twig left and right,
"Shaplacky, Shaplacky!" with his widdly wand.

The water started to sizzle,
It seemed to be on fire.
He then flicked his wand yet again,
And the water quickly became this man's attire.

He then snickered as a child would,
Jumping so high in mighty hops.
He then looked over to me with joy,
As when I stumbled hitting my head, he said "Widdly, Widdly Wop!"

I awoke from my sleep that night,

(Shaplacky, shaplacky, I hummed!)
That was all just a dream, I thought!?
Until I felt my head, which sat a pretty good lump.

"Sun-light vs. Night-Moon"

Rise, says the moon to the sun,
I am sleepy too!
I wish to fall asleep during your shine,
So I extend my audience to you.
Where are you?
It is half past your scheduled a.m.
I know where I am,
But as for you, I do not!
Have you forgotten you rise sooner now,
Or have you again forgot?

"Here I am!" say's the Sun to the Moon;
Don't get all worked up, because when you do,
You just look like a silly Buffoon!
Me, on the other hand, I still feel a little tired.
So watch the world for me a while longer,
So that I can rest my weary eye-fire.

No, says the Moon.
I will not do your work any longer.
I have had enough of the combustions of excuses.
Excuse me, says the Sun!
I am not making excuses or refusing to do my job.
I am merely telling you, you must,
You have no other choice!
Otherwise, I will scorch your surface in flames-
Without rejoice, so sustain!

I am brightness, says the light,

So you better take note you round Moon.
I and the Sun are great kings,
While you are just plainly a Moon.

Hold on! I am black says the night,
And you two shall do no such thing.
Because If you both do, there will be nothing left.
Then only I shall reign!

"Fly Fingers, Fly!"

I'm slowly walking-
Down the road of concrete dreams.
Long it seems!
I am just dreaming-
Forever on a milky skyway of chocolate highways,
Thinking of richer schemes.
I am shouting with my hands held high,
As my fingertips discuss no meaning,
For they are birds in the sun, just beginning their flight.
My index is a dove and my pinky is a crane,
So they are flying in harmony-
All as one, without pain.
I flutter those fingers of mine into the wind-
And begin to swim my limbs.
Now I am flying;
Just soaring like a butterfly.
I am high,
Deeper into the suns skyline.
I am now walking-
Down the road of cloudy dreams.
Soft they seem,
But I am no longer dreaming,
Rather living amongst those clouds-
Which feel of soft-like teases.

These fingers of mine have feathers,
And they able me with flight.
I can dabble them in any weather,
And yet still take on the night.

"Shooting Star"

I sat and wondered one night,
Who am I, I thought?
So profoundly then had shined a light,
Touching my skin so nice;
It was such a mystical hue of wrought.
All of my fingers were then gleaming,
My eyes were so spacey,
And my body was glistening.
I thought I was just dreaming,
Or perhaps going crazy!

I took both my index and thumb-
And I then pinched my skin;
It hurt only some,
But next to none,
I was not dreaming, rather glowing brighter from within!

I then planted my feet apart
And I jumped so very high,
Elevating amongst other stars,
So afar;
I just couldn't believe thine eyes!

So apart from all the stars,
I think maybe this night, I too shine.
How far, oh how far-
They all are;
Their beauty I now borrow as mine.

"The Last Path Home"

I once completed a journey.
This expedition was long and intricate.
When I came to this pass by a lake,
There were so many paths I could take;
I only wished for I to duplicate.

There were so many lefts,
Which meant, so many wrong turns.
And so many rights,
Furthermore meant, only one to be right.
The exact way home was too discerned.

I watched as I wondered,
While others repeatedly had passed.
They all seemed to not care much-
For their path and of it's such;
They were a step shy from a dash.

I was so confused,
But more so just afraid.
So I spun all around in circles,
Then stopped and straightforward I hurtled-
Without questioning my way.

I sprinted so very fast;
Even though I ran alone,
I began to recollect those people which beside me came.
And as our trails were but the same.
I found out that all paths would ultimately lead home.

"Looking Back as a Cloud"

How has this come to be?
This feeling, this moment
Of me in front of me?
With ponder, I wondered
Among the unending wonder
Of the answers I need for me.

Lying in the grass I stare
At the clouds and I see-
A reflection of me there,
Just as a cloud,
Dressed in white shroud,
So high, way up there!

It was there I glanced back at me.
So peculiar are those eyes-
I thought; blanketing a willow tree-
With the sadness in a soul-
Of which no one truly knows;
The saddest of all the trees.

But there I am,
Just me in front of thee-
Doing all a cloud-me can,
Giving away my smiles
To that me which hasn't in a while,
To smile again, again, and again!

"Broken-Wolf"

High up on a mountain,
A tribe brings forth a slowly child in his youth;
A boy nearly changed into his aged seasons.

The eldest wise man said unto him,
"Boy, now it is time for your vision quest,
So may you find your true mind within it."

From the first opening of his ears,
The child has been told of the spirits;
How they would come to him and appear,
To aid him on his way,
But to find them, he must go so far and away.

Afraid and alone, the boy ventured from that mountain,
Away from his home,
Absent to the eyes of those who loved him.
Into the wild, a world to him that is unknown,
He journeyed on to find himself.

No fare to be with his mouth.
No delight to be upon his tongue.
Only aroma within his snout,
As well as an empty fragrance to sip and slake.

Late into the night,
Twelve moons had come and gone-
As starvation has made its way,
Lacking the might within his arms-
To go on, on to the next break of day.

As the sun broke through the horizon,
His eyes expanded into dull range;
Unresponsive to the worlds astral light,
His appetite, he could no longer sustain.

Nature then grew eyes and gazed-
As the sun withdrew,
Escaping his eyes from the day;
Unraveling and untying-
The final moon for the child to envisage.

Time was frozen,
With all twelve moons to the sky.
A sprite then fell in feathered motion,
Circling around the boy,
As he danced and played underneath the spirits eyes.

As the sprite grounded dirt,
A ripple emitted a wave within all nature.
The glow began to take shape of a sitting wolf,
As it looked to the boy with such overwhelming favor.

The wolf noticed the boys slowly mind,
How it was broken,
And many years so left behind;
So he howled, yowling to the twelve moons in the sky.

The wolfs song was of understanding and sympathy,
For the stars were not properly aligned.
The stars then began to rearrange and sustained-
More distinction within that child's defeated mind.

The twelve moons then counted down with disappearance,
And with the last moon, the wolf rose to his feet.
Standing sound in mind and spirit,
The wolf released to that child a light never so deep.
The child then arose, dead to the world,
Now in understanding of which was not before.
He cried tears of joy,
For he was now a bright young boy-
More so ever times four.
Journeying back home, he gave homage to the spirits,
And thanked the wolf for his broken mind now restored.

-The Color Yellow- Act V

Out of all the colors, shades, and blush, the brightest of them all comes at dusk; and with it comes, "Beauty".

"I, the Pianist"

When the world turns over, covering me in shade,
I sit upon a stool outside, without reflection of the present.
I just stare at the stars and shape the night as if clay,
Thus, my rendition begins to play;
Envisaging ivories of pattern to form an instrument.

I then play thy piano keys.
And with these strokes, I can manifest my way.
There be not a place, to which now I more see
Than these black and white keys, suitably placed in front of me,
As the rhythmic tunes cleverly sooth out the day.

With these hands, I am the grand pianist, I am the imposing design.
I construct the tides of thy life;
And what is more, my heart has intertwined with the key-strokes of
my sublime,
Evermore raining opulence in the grandeur of thine night.

"Lady Weather"

Winter, summer, spring, and fall,
They're all the expressions of lady weather.
Whether withered amid thunder-flings, held in thrall;
She is a lady, without cleave to a fetter.

Finesse is utterance and spoken by very many,
Because she is the wind and all.
Copious in natures plenty,
She is the temperate winds, she is the feral squall.

She is the clement lightning; she is the strident thunder,
And where she rests in slumber fashions a cold night.
Her silky textured skin never bares any blunder,

As she sets loose a watcher; a loving, tender sprite.

She is the lady of all things pleasant;
The illustration of a true beauty,
And she is the magic in the field of essence,
Who's perfumed in all things fruity.

She is the coy in smirk-less eyes
Who bears of flake-like water;
The one who brings you change, who I-
Happen to love, named charming lady weather.

"Serendipity Within"

Over eager feet,
You rarely know where they go.
Under eager scenes
Never get seen,
So in time they deplete,
Thus, are never shown.

As the modern-scenic paintings more so cover,
Sheathing the countless possibilities,
Forming a loss to dreams
More so leans
Towards the ex-lover
Of harsh cold reality.

Serendipity simply means,
All in all, just magic;
The discovered path to logic,
A well-known subject
Of which counts on dreams,
For great minds just to grab it!

"Rain Down On Me"

The clouds are beginning to form;
I see no other path home,
So I must walk my way forlorn.
But I hold no dwelling; I am but a man standing there alone.
That place I had never known,
It's as painful as a thorn.

The clouds grow more in length and width,
The touch of radiance stirs every follicle.
The feeling of empty rift-
Deepens within this heart of no domicile;
It is all too futile,
Like climbing a climbless cliff.

If I walk in this rain that now falls,
I shall be plenty soaked.
Maybe, just maybe I won't stall;
I might not even need a coat,
As I am already abundantly cloaked-
In tears of tasteless salt.

Stepping into the storm, I take my deepest breath…
I smile and leave it all behind,
While dripping of nervous sweat.
I say this storm is mine,
And it is here I will find-
Peace, the beauty in nothing left.

Walking amongst these raindrops,
I feel it wrapping my body as if a child.
I hope this never stops,
Because this, right here and now-
Is all worth the while,
And I like it a lot.

But still though, my thoughts were corrupt.
(I have no place to call home)
Then the clouds called a bluff,
Forming such amazing cyclones,
While raging their furious tones;
Oh how this was all just beautiful enough!

There for, I shouted to those gusts of winds,
"Come, rain down on me-
And wipe away all these sins,
Set me free!"
I then felt a strongly breeze
Striking my body as if pricks of pins.

The rain poured and reigned as if a king,
And implored me to turn back.
It voiced to me, "You should know of no such thing!"
I begged to feel what I lacked,
As then, in came thunder cracks;
I wanted to go home, to them I sang!

Suddenly, strikes of lighting flashed,
They clapped and they struck-
Deep into my body, lifting me past-
My feet which were stuck;
As I then blasted into the sky, straight up;
Now I am home at last!

"Resting Tide to Nirvana"

The seasons are changing
And so am I, but they are recurring,
But no not I.
For I am clocked in,
Pending a closure to my eyes.

My skin is becoming paper;
Rough, as it's harder to sustain cater
To my etched creases and stains,
So I say, "See you later,
I am going into my wane."

I lived most of my life like water,
Just peacefully sauntered.
So I lay upon this shoreline
Thinking of the holy wonders;
How I would greet them in due time.

As I converge my sending point,
Losing the feeling within my joints,
And my voice lacks its tone;
The heavens appoint,-
I can finally close my eyes and let the tide take me home.

"Windowsill Dreams"

Beside my window, I fell asleep;
A backwards meaning,
Because out there I'm dreaming,
I am not just asleep.
I feel like I am flying,
I could not cease supplying
Those thoughts, these scenes, this plot.
I don't want to leave,
For this beauty is my sleeve;
Without it, I am naught!
I dream and I dream,
Without a peep, not a peep,
So wake me no more,
And let me explore
My eternal dream sleep.

"Desk on a Beach"

My desk by water sits,
Standing accompanied by my stool.
It is all just beautiful enough-
To keep me absent minded, but not a fool.

The rhythmic beat of water is splashing
As I sit still, ever silent.
The sand pebbles sneak their way-
Cleverly between my toes, and I circumvent.

The birds are singing will all joy,
For not a thing was wrong today.
This day and this moment,
I orchestrate my artist's heart away.

This desk is my third eyed window,
And the wind has become my pen.
I have lost my former self-
To the humbleness in beauty's accent.

Through the days and nights I remain there in harmony,
In the ever glaze of simpler things.
And as my eyes are placed upon the horizon,
I and my desk by water transform all that needs change.

"In Insanity, There in Beauty"

In all that is beyond
And forthcoming, we-
But see the present inclinations.
When we open what is called neon-
Lighting from a bottle, I believe-
It all to be a hidden agenda, a sleeping procreation-

Which knows a color to be red, which is true;
Although with mind's eye we can alter it into translucent blue.

So, to see beyond the wellness of an easy mind
Is to influence finer schematics
To be drawn.
The sanity we then leave behind,
Causes a rhythmic tic-
Of views into our more beautiful designs,
Hence, we can dream up richer schemes
For the beauty in all lesser things.

"Windshield Waltz"

Side-to-side, they stray all the rain
Away like a tide,
Ebbing what the glass has claimed;
The drip drops from the sky.

Left to right, they hold repetition,
Like a voice returned with echo
And all its dimensions,
To come back once again, and again be let go.

Side-to-side they stand,
Like a duet of music drums.
A composed marching band,
As it heart beats upon each thump.

Left to right, they rock
To the click of our liking.
And not once do they complain or stop,
They just keep steady wiping.

"Underneath the Skin"

True beauty lies only within itself,
Not of any tricks or deceitful paintings.
The pure justice in one that is felt
Will not dishearten the skin in which you came in

Every scar that bares vision holds a tale,
Sometimes chronically among innate;
A secret not told, but sheltered in veil.
The true beauty in you is the given of a face.

Underneath it all, you may have wings,
In which wait to blossom giving flight
Like a bird or cascade of many things.
I find tonight, in which my skin shines so bright.

"Water-Balloon Fight"

To steal a day away with splendor so nice,
Is the greatest of pleasures,
One of the greatest delights.
This sport has no measure,
It is but a fight
Of water and rubber;
A clever game quite,
With glee and some wonder,
A water-balloon fight.

"Temple of Beauty"

I am at one within my thoughts.
I am an adjunct gust to the winds.
And I fear not of where I sought,
As my true beauty lies within.

I am water and I am fire;
Together, I suppress and express
My entire splendor as a choir,
Deepening my harmony as I transgress.

I close my eyes within my mind
And I envision a perfect state of self.
Inside I must quickly climb-
The open arms and hands of hell.

I then propel myself into the air,
And I jump afar the proffers which lure.
I am flawed perfectly within to err,
Floating among thy ground of pure.

Finally comes the light of prominence
To excel its celestial duties;
Draping curtains over all the malevolence,
Roaring simple undying beauty.

"All My Life"

So far it has been a struggle,
But here I still am.
My existence is still present-
Because of the strength in which god demands.
The crescent moon reflects my life tonight.
I have lived without love for half of that,

As now I am fuller than a starlit light.
All of my life, I sat and watched the skies pass to days-
Unto darkened faint.
Now my breath is as free as the birds of summer;
I feel so exotically quaint!
Still I am here, and that surprises me,
For these reasons I state:
I am a man who has shed tears, you see?
Does that make me less of a man-
Since I have supplied the abundance of a salty sea?
I highly doubt that a man cannot cry,
Because all of my life I have fought my demons and tried.
I am joyous now, and still I am here,
Along with my lips which now so happily curl;
I have waited all of my life for this smile to appear!

"Jabberwocky"

Up is dawn,
And left is height,
Down is songs,
And right just might.

In front is behind,
And the skies are the ground,
The sea is sublime,
And hither is all around.

My eyes feel it all,
And I see the feeling.
My tongue smells raw,
As my nose speaks meaning.

I am here,
So, here am I,

And I reappear;
Appearing without eyes!

Back is front,
Now front is back,
I want, I want-
A ration of snacks!

Talking without sense;
So senseless without talking.
Words are dispensed,
Hence, I am just jabberwocking!

"Every Waken Moment"

At the quarter of five, my eyes rise
As I get out my bed to heed bird cries.
I then up my window to view the world that's outside;
With my eyes that are open, I feel it's all mine.
Taking a deep breath, I consume the pure land
Before the world wakes and takes from its given hands,
With then the courage and strength of ten men;
I close these eyes now to whisper, "Yes I can."

As I wash away the day before, I feel cleansed,
While smiling with a little patience that god had sent,
Along with some inspiration, I'm sure he meant,
That his words shall protect me; to I he fends.

Once ready in all ways, I look to the mirror
And I see me today, as a man who looks clearer;
Beyond the skies of my eyes to own no fear,
But only clutch the dreams in which I hold dear.

With the silence of what I see,

I feel the entire world here and connected to me.
And when you know not of what you be,
You can become anything your mind fathoms you to dream.

Finally, when I am ready for this trance of day,
I embrace it all with reverie I hold today.
And when nothing left is more to say,
I walk out that door to become, and dream I may.

"Set Free"

When eyes rise above chilled shade,
Your heart is set free from its holding cage;
Away from the walk into a quick blade,
And into the light of no more fade.

Your destiny is nothing but a vision felt;
A cabinetry of truth, and nothing else.
It deals you peace and makes you melt
From the love unkempt, held around your belt.

In a world where truth is told,
Truth be the only thing in which I know.
Once a feeling in which I loathed,
Now I know which way I go.

I go to a place, in which I shine,
The only place, in which stays mine;
A dream, a thought of once a time;
Living and loving became my design.

I am happy, because still I'm here.
I shed no more worries from these tears.
And, to rise faster than all my fears
Has been the greatest happen in all my years.

"A Hidden World"

Raindrops on drums play silent symphonies
While in engagement of tacit conclusions
Of maybe a world that is sure next to me;
It's all baffling to know of these hidden illusions.

It makes me wonder of what is there
As it shows itself in hidden agendas,
Only to disappear without a care;
It leaves one to ask among a bard stanza,

What be of this second existence?
To feel something so close, I can imagine,
And reach into the shadows of its symptoms,
Playing among the world of fathom.

"Everybody's Free"

Together, this night we make glorious tribute among the stars,
And we shall walk on heavens white carpet in peace,
For only our sins have kept us bound in eternal bars;
A truth in which we now shout from desolate knees.

We have to be free…
For in our hearts we journey where whosesoever shall kindly see us,
And give us the pure joy of a smile to feel good in who we be.
In what feeling can endure more than love, can be just?

Into the open arms of light, let us lay down our robes
And spend our last breath upon this beautiful land.
We are in true awe of this beauty that we have come to know,
Now let us be returned forever into freedoms hands.

"Farewell thy Garden"

Among all of the words and syllables to be said,
I choose to say goodbye to thy garden.
I am not a complicated guy, but simple instead;
I am just the witty man with flowers to give me pardon.

I am now in the glory of the lord.
As I am gone presently, I share another type of beauty.
So do not be sad my garden, as our maker has given me ward,
And the best of all is that he has given me a very special duty.

While I was in heaven, I had felt a little hurt;
For my flowers who be left behind, are mislaid to another.
As then god had appeared; I knew of what not to assert.
He then had asked me so kind to blossom his great wonders.

As for now, I am just a wondering man in the heavens of outside,
Planting a fresh garden, so please do not cry.
Just wipe the dew away from thee eyes,
And if you shall need me, just look to thine sky.

So now it is time to say goodbye to the garden that I adored;
Farewell to the brilliance in which I awaited.
To my wife and kids, all of many four;
You are the most beautiful garden I had ever created.

"The Stars Will Carry On"

Under the blankets of our lidded vision,
Our modest looking glasses;
We can see and witness dotted glare.
Some are brighter than the next,
While others merely are far fair.

The masters of the cosmos,
Where punctured darkness emits rivulets of light,
Establishing claim to all that has remained,
Before time itself and its dawn of first life.

Diamonds are in the sky.
Luminous and dazzling they are,
But why?
The backdrop of invariable change
Is of grace, as those stars are meticulously arranged
To never variate or exchange its resting place.

The scriptures of time itself must be there,
Linking the characters able for alignment to watch over,
To protect, and to give us awe;
Given by our king, but we carried on and annulled
The ordinance of beauty in the night we so stare.

I ask you starry sky,
Please look past our selfishness to woo under you,
Not flattering your eyes;
Giving you thanks for unchanging loyalty.
Our dormant hearts seem to think you are there for us,
Although, we will pass with time and you will persist,
Leaving left only you.

"Restless Midnight"

The heart is a piano,
As one keystroke could all suffice.
Midnight is when it is purest,
Amongst the nestle of blackened ripe.

When the world rests their weary eyes,
I am taken into flight;

I am higher than all the skies,
And have taken this dreamful night!

So be this the only knowing I have;
The truth in every hour rests amongst no sleep,
And as the time devours,
Thine eyes do not mournful weep.

Thus, the pain has forgotten me,
And conflictions rest the mind.
So midnight has my suspicions,
That it is there you can leave it all behind!

When that clock strikes one or two,
You know you have to leave;
To sleep means you must go,
For next amorrows so doings please.

Goodnight to you midnight;
You are my wakened feat-
By far!
I'll see you again in my restless midnight sleep!

"Sweet Departure"

Standing by an ocean,
On-looking all of the pretty blue-
Is where I await something,
Something I had never knew.

Under sun-fire and rhombus elusory stars,
I remain, awaiting something great.
Onward I look so far,
Scoping the horizons for my longing fate.

Out there on the ocean,
No bridges are found, only distance;
But somewhere under the clouds, there is hope, and-
I on-look in the offing, where the water decides to glisten.

Standing in unspoken glance,
I am outnumbered by the mass of sand;
Does finding one unique pebble really resemble my chance?
If so, I will still look-on with all I can.

Sitting upon the waves,
The surge comes rushing to my fingers in taunt,
As I sketch this sunset which holds me enslaved-
To hold on, bear on, and linger on.

Out there is where I gaze at,
Where the cloak of colors reflect like mirrors;
Showing only my reflection looking back,
Mimicking the faith I govern sitting here.

Laying upon the ocean,
I widen my eyes to the half-circle of display.
Still I await that something,
While taking in final beauty, before my eyes are flayed.

Awaiting for the ocean,
I look so far past the horizon.
I so contentedly smiled, deciding then;
This is where the sky and my eyes must end.

Now adrift upon the ocean,
My eyes and body's warmth embodies no one;
Although, my heart and soul embarked with nothing,
I feel my ship has finally come…

"Sunset"

Akin to men and shores, the sun again lays to rest.
And as equivalent to times on-board,
A fisherman has seen the test;
The wonders of Poseidon,
Among his vast sea at best.
Now the subsiding comes to dividing,
A world of timely roars.
The dark and the light shall unite brightly dressed,
To dazzle thine eyes and yours;
To keep and never forget-
This sunset that befits my shore;
This is true beauty, I attest!

For Angel...

"Within every new morning comes your new face in the mirror; it is there you decide who you will be."

~Michael J.H. Messiano~

www.ingramcontent.com/pod-product-compliance
Ingram Content Group UK Ltd.
Pitfield, Milton Keynes, MK11 3LW, UK
UKHW041939190726
13854UKWH00004B/1672

9 781257 623105